A Pioneer *in* Patagonia

Don Santiago de Larminat, 1910

Miguel de Larminat

A Pioneer
in Patagonia

The Remarkable Life
of Santiago de Larminat

*For Simon and Yvonne
hoping to see you again
in Patagonia*

Feb. 2014

Ⓐ **Editorial El Ateneo**

De Larminat, Miguel María
  A pioneer in Patagonia : The remarkable life of Santiago de Larminat/ con colaboración de: Andrew Graham-Yooll - 1a. ed. - Buenos Aires : El Ateneo, 2005.
  296 p. ; 24x17 cm.

  Traducido por: Daniel Ginhson

  ISBN 950-02-5934-6

  1. De Larminat, Santiago-Biografía I. Graham-Yooll, Andrew, colab. II. Daniel Ginhson, trad. III. Título
  CDD 923.

A pioneer in Patagonia. The remarkable life of Santiago de Larminat
Título original: Un pionero de la Patagonia
© 2005, Miguel de Larminat
Translated from the Spanish by Daniel Ginhson
Reviewed by Andrew Graham-Yooll

Graphic Design: Eduardo Ruiz

Primera edición de Editorial El Ateneo
© 2005, Grupo ILHSA S.A.
  Patagones 2463 - (C1282ACA) , Buenos Aires, Argentina
  E-mail: editorial@elateneo.com
ISBN 950-02-5934-6

Printed by Printing Books, Mario Bravo 835, Avellaneda, provincia de Buenos Aires, Argentina, in June 2005

Printed in Argentina

ACKNOWLEDGEMENTS

Juan Pablo and Cecilia Correa, who had faith in this project from the
    start. Without their optimism and encouragement, I would not
    have been able to produce this book.
César Aira, who helped me shape the draft in form and quality.
My book designer, Eduardo Ruiz, who kept smiling in spite of the
    last minute changes.
Aunts Jacqueline, Simone and Rosa Ana, who supplied me with
    information and support, and aunt Michelle, who helped me with
    the photographs.
María Ana de Larminat, who gave me the wealth of her memories.
Aunt Jeanine, who allowed me to reproduce my grandfather's water-
    colors.
Christine de Larminat, who sent her aunt Paule's memoirs, Bruno de
    Larminat, who helped find our family's path in France, and René
    de Larminat, who opened his archives.
Pascal de Cugnac, who worked on the picture scanning process.
Bonifacio del Carril, who always encouraged me, and wrote the jack-
    et notes.
Andrew Graham-Yooll, who helped me with the english version.
My parents, who supported me throughout this project.
My wife Isabel and my children, Victoria and Pablo, who endured
    long hours in front of the computer.

Don Santiago de Larminat, 1954

INTRODUCTION

*T*HIS IS MY GRANDFATHER'S LIFE; JACQUES de Larminat, *don*[1] Santiago. Although it is the story of a man and his family, it is, to a certain extent, the history of Patagonia and of its pioneers, and consequently a part of the history of Argentina.

The severe and benevolent figure of my grandfather, *Bon Papa*, as we called him, was present throughout my childhood and youth, and has borne a lasting influence on many aspects of my life. I see him, in what I believe is my first recollection of him, coming out of the main entrance of his home with his brother Esteban, descending the three steps from the veranda; it was summertime, and the enormous weeping willow which provided shade over the front door seemed to quiver under the merciless sun in the Andean foothills. It must have been on a Sunday after lunch, as that was when he often came out and sat on one of the benches in front of the house, to enjoy the sight of his beloved trees and of the Lanín volcano, which could still be seen then from that spot. Later on this view was cut off by the foliage, and nobody dared cut down the trees to restore the imposing prospect.

---

[1] Originally, De Origen Noble (Of Noble Birth), a Spanish title of respect, later used popularly before the given name.

Around 1955, when I was five years old, there were four main houses on the *estancia*. In the center of the homestead, on the right margin of the Chimehuin river, my grandfather's house stood out as the main construction. Close to it was ours, and further out my uncle Bernardo's. Bernardo and Andrés –my father– were don Santiago's eldest children, the only males. Across the river, very close to the place where many years later I built my own house, my great-uncle Esteban had his home. My grandfather's and Esteban's houses had been built in the twenties, and remained a silent testimony of the circumstances endured by the heroic settlers. The buildings were made entirely of wood, painted white with a shade of ocher, with roofs and outside skirt-boards a sealing-wax color.

With my grandfather and my grandmother Magdalena, a beautiful lady with snow white hair and eyes an incredibly deep blue, lived five of my aunts, all single: Jacqueline, Simone, Jeanine, Rose Anne and Michelle. A sixth aunt, Guillemette, had married Jacques Pesme, a Frenchman from Morocco, where they had settled. Three daughters of my great-uncle Esteban and his wife Geneviève lived with them; they were Claire, Alix and Thérèse. Their son Jean was in Buenos Aires, and their eldest daughter, Elisabeth, had married an *estanciero*[2] of Basque origin, don Andrés Laxague, and lived in Coronel Pringles, in the province of Buenos Aires, devoted to the production of children (they had nineteen) and of grain. Two other sisters, Monique and Odile, were studying to become Benedictine nuns.

Uncle Bernardo's house, like ours, was made of carved stone, with a roof of wooden tiles painted red, the style which later was followed in all constructions on the *estancia*. Bernardo and his wife Manina had ten children, and at about that time the first had been born: María Ana, a great friend of mine, and Eduardo, my brother Pedro's contemporary and pal.

---

[2] A country gentleman, owner of an *estancia*.

Mercedes, Verónica and Carlos, were still tiny. Later on came Nicolás, María Elena, Luis Enrique, María Susana and Cecilia. As for us, we were only three.

There was never a lack of children, particularly in the summer holidays, when the Laxague cousins arrived, and also the cousins on my mother's side, the Iribarrens (Claude, Paul and Pifi), who were older than us but excellent playmates and friends, and who brought with them their own acquaintances.

In 1956, when France withdrew from Morocco, the Pesmes came to stayon the *estancia* for a couple of years. At that time the Pesmes had only three children –Olivier, Chantal and little Xavier– later increasing that number to seven, following the prolific tradition of the family. A cousin of Bernardo's, pretty Christine Hansen, also joined the crowd.

Such an army of children favored the organization of games of all kinds. Factory-made toys were never necessary, as the immense riches that nature put at our disposal were more than enough for us. Memories abound of huge picnics, swimming in the Chimehuin, horseback rides, days spent working with the cattle, barbecues and camping, battles fought with wooden swords, bows and arrows, the conquest of woods and hills which had fallen into enemy hands, persecutions at full gallop over the huge property...

Proof of our ability to manage without buying things is shown by the story that follows.

I remember that the Iribarrens had the habit of staying for a few days at the home of cousins Laxague, in Coronel Pringles, before arriving at our house.

The Laxagues received many French publications, and among them the latest books of cartoons of a character who afterwards became famous, the Belgian originated journalist Tintin and his dog Milou. My cousins Iribarren, and particularly Paul, loved the stories of Tintin and Milou, and each year, as soon as they arrived at the Laxagues, read the latest issues time and again with such zeal that they practically learned them by heart.

Over at Cerro de los Pinos we waited anxiously for Paul's arrival, as his memory was the best, and begged him tell us the latest Tintin adventures, which each year became more and more exciting. We Larminats had no access to those books, as our parents would not buy such frivolities, much less considering their price in French francs. Paul was a superb storyteller, and had us and my cousins hanging from his every word. He even made drawings of the settings, including the rockets to the moon and the pocket submarines that Tintin used to explore space or to go and recover a treasure on some islands in the Pacific. This was a true case of oral tradition in the twentieth century, and the whole process was so precise that we even organized competitions to see which one of us knew by heart the names of all the characters, and could describe more accurately the settings of each episode. In the long run we managed to convince our parents to buy the books, and so, the competitions became even more demanding.

1

*My Grandfather
in my Recollections*

Don Santiago and the author, 1954

*I*N MY MEMORY I SEE MY GRANDFATHER coming out of the house wearing a light jacket, a battered cotton hat and woolen spats. He normally dressed in light beige colors. His brother Esteban, slightly older, preferred a range of gray and a more elegant hat. as he became older, my grandfather began to use cotton drill trousers, made by Grafa, but at that time he still used those woolen spats, just like Esteban. They both looked very much alike, and sported a similar white moustache, but my grandfather had a much heftier build, plus an amazing likeness with Albert Einstein. He swayed in his gait, he was bow-legged and moved his arms as if to help him keep his balance, but this fact did not deter him from walking several kilometers each day.

Esteban, never too keen on physical exertion, was more inclined to intellectual matters. He was an engineer by profession, and had taken upon himself the task of furnishing the estancia with the necessary equipment. In the years of my childhood he had ceased to work, and led a simple life. He had chosen to reside on the northern shore of the Chimehuin, a very isolated place in those times. My great-aunt, being a very sociable person, resented this decision.

We called my grandfather's house the Old House.

Ours was about a hundred meters away, and when we children went over to see them, my grandmother's and my aunts' welcome was invariably happy and cheerful. My grandparents' bedroom was warm and cozy; it had large windows, its walls were paneled with beech, decorated with tapestries made by Mapuche[1] indians in shades of brown, black and white, and had an imposing three-door wardrobe with an oval mirror in the middle. On the walls hung watercolors painted by my

Magdelon de Larminat

grandfather, and there was a photograph of him and our grandmother with all of their children, in which my father and uncle Bernardo appeared in military uniform, plus several religious pictures.

My grandmother was sweet-tempered and professed devotion to her husband. She found everything he did to be excellent, and that must have been the formula for their married happiness. With her grandchildren she was affectionate and fun-loving; she used to read to us stories that she had kept from her own childhood. Among them were some written by Countess de Ségur, books bound in pale rose-colored cloth with golden lettering, where the exhilarating adventures of Sophie, the author's grandchild, were told. Countess de Ségur's grandparents had been Russian, and had lived on the land just like us. As for my aunts, they contributed their joy and originality;

[1] Mapuche: Tribal name of the Araucanian native people

several of them had a fine hand for drawing, and also painted watercolors. I remember my aunt Jacqueline produced some bookbinding
in leather which I thought beautiful. My grandfather, would join us
once he was through with his daily work.

Don Santiago's conversation was always interesting and instructive. He had no time for small talk; whatever he said had a clear purpose. Quite often the line he chose to follow drove conversations to
matters totally different and unexpected, but they were invariably
original and creative. He and my grandmother, following a family
tradition, were fervent, open minded Catholics. I remember that the
great French religious writers were held in high regard at home:
Fénelon, Bossuet, Pascal, Claudel. My grandmother's family had
been distinguished by an ancestor, Father Jogue, a Jesuit who died at
the hands of the Iroquois in Québec, Canada, where he had gone to
catechize, in the times of Louis XV. The death of this ancestor was
pictured in an engraving that puzzled us; he appeared half-naked,
tied to a stake amid flames and surrounded by North American Indians. My grandmother used to tell us this story while we, open-
mouthed, kept our eyes fixed on the engraving; while grandfather
deplored Louis XV's unwitting decision to sell Canada to England,
after describing the colony derisively as *"quelques arpents de neige"*
(some hectares of snow).

During my early childhood my grandfather would gather round
him the eldest among us and enthrall us with stories that were a selection from La Fontaine's fables and narrations from French lore,
which he had written in notebooks illustrated with watercolors.
Sometimes he would give us a sheet of paper with a drawing on one
side, and the story written on the reverse. He also had in his reperto-
ry Greek and Roman myths, anecdotes from the Great War –in
which he had taken part– and accounts of his travels in Argentina and
around the world.

In summertime all our games were played outdoors. I particularly remember a very popular wooden hippopotamus, made by

one of my grandfather's brothers (I think it was Robert) for his children, which could be mounted and ridden holding on to its ears, which were made of leather. This animal had been constructed with tongue-and-groove jointed wood painted a brilliant pearl gray, and the head, with the nose a sealing-wax color, could be moved up and down, something we enjoyed tremendously. During winter we played with wooden blocks in a little room by my grandparents' bedroom, where don Santiago had painted on the aquamarine wall a series of African animals in red and black which went all the way across the ceiling. We would observe them without really believing that those animals existed. In our Patagonian mountains it was difficult for us to imagine, giraffes, monkeys, rhinoceros, elephants and zebras. The knitting machine was in that room, a contraption which seemed to me of enormous proportions, and where my grandmother would sometimes sit to knit pullovers.

On other occasions we would be taken to the first floor, to "the Classroom", so called because it was the room where my father and his brother and sisters had received tuition before going to school in Buenos Aires. Beside "the Classroom" my aunts had their own room, where my grandfather had also painted animals and scenes that went over the ivory-colored wall and across the ceiling. The pictures illustrated French popular songs, such as "Sur le Pont d'Avignon", "A la Claire Fontaine", "Le Vieux Moulin" or "Le Roi Dagobert".

Later my cousins, my brother and I would also take lessons, with my aunts and my grandfather as teachers, in addition to my mother, who taught us Spanish and managed our progress as external pupils at the school in San Martín de los Andes. With my elder cousins María Ana and Eduardo, and my brother Pedro, we took courses in French primary schooling at our grandfather's.

This was so until the arrival of governesses, the "Mademoiselles", who played the roles of my father's and his siblings' "Mademoiselles" with a difference of thirty years.

The Old House

Those early years of learning were very special, and recalling them I cannot but feel admiration at the way my grandfather was able to capture the attention and interest of the six and seven-year olds he taught. His subjects were history and geography, and also Latin, a language he loved and in which he had been thoroughly instructed. Years later, when I already had a French tutor, Mademoiselle Lafleur des Pois, whenever my grandfather traveled to Europe we corresponded in Latin. I remember the long arguments I had with Mademoiselle Lafleur when I, at age eleven, wrote to don Santiago telling him that I had been given a .22 caliber carbine. Should I decline the word "carbine"? And if so, in which declination? In the first, as in "rosa, rosae, rosam"? Then it should be "carabina, carabinae, carabinam..." We finally decided against any declination.

My grandfather's tuition was driven by his love of nature, which made his lectures on geography and geology alluring . Pursuant to his keen sense of observation he was able to provide the most vivid and attractive descriptions. Trees, rivers, lakes, mountains, everything became alive in his words and in his drawings. And above all, stones. Geology was not included in school programs, but it was important for him; he used to bring from the fields samples of quartz, feldspar, granite, limestone, petrified trunks and fossils, to show us their characteristics and differences, as well as their usefulness and beauty.

No less was the interest that his history lectures aroused in us. He would not restrict himself to the official programs, and probably ignored their existence. He spoke to us about what he considered examples to follow in life, and, what made his teaching more exciting, he did not limit himself to the real or supposed mental standards of seven-year olds. I vividly remember his incursions into Greek and Roman mythology, which sparked my intereset in those gods and goddesses that he described with such humor and originality, that has lasted to this day. The Trojan war, the Iliad and the Odyssey, Hercules' labors, the Aeneid, were stories that lasted hours and days, and which always held the suspense through to the next sitting.

The same happened with the accounts of the kings of France, who marched before our eyes century after century, and about whom he had very firm views. Some had been good, others bad; there had been progressive princes and poor rulers. I specially recall the detailed description of Louis XI, who at that time was portrayed in textbooks as a cruel and mean sovereign; for my grandfather, in contrast, he had been one of the most important kings in the history of France. Fifteen years later his opinion was endorsed by a memorable book written by the North American historian Paul M. Kendall. Grandfather also admired Louis XIV, while disapproving of his squandering of public monies on sumptuous constructions, such as Versailles. On the other hand he despised the unfortunate Louis XVI, "a weakling dominated by his wife, totally incapable of assuming his role as Head of State". Obviously the last of the Capetians was not up to the standard of my grandfather's patriarchal guidelines.

Santiago de Larminat with his grandchildren:
Pedro, Mercedes, the author and Marie Anne

Don Santiago also used to tell us about European history of the late nineteenth and early twentieth centuries, with the passion of one who had taken part in events. Although he and his brother fought against Germany in the Great War, he kept a surprisingly open mind on that country. He considered Germany a natural ally of France, much more than England, a power which to him was subject to its own short-term interests and consequently deserving little trust. He always called England "perfidious Albion", recalling the brutal exploitation of workers in the English mines in Queen Victoria's times. He admired count Bismarck, and, closer to our own times, Adenauer, the architect with de Gaulle of the formidable enterprise that was the European Coal and Steel Community, which would develop eventually into the European Community.

With De Gaulle he had a peculiar love hate relationship: he admitted his status as a statesman, his vision and his heroism when France capitulated, in 1940, but he was worried by De Gaulle's links with the left,

25

and he questioned the inclusion of Communist ministers in the coalition government of 1945.

Another subject on which he would elaborate with pleasure was the French colonial empire. We would listen enthralled to his stories about the conquests in north Africa, in Indochina and especially in the heart of Africa, with the battles between the Germans, the French and the British. The names of captain Marchand and the Fashoda incident, of sheik Abd-el-Kader, Livingston and Stanley, and naturally Marshall Lyautey, awoke in our children's minds the excitment of mystery and adventure.

When my grandfather considered Argentine history he did so from of his political beliefs, and with the hopes with which he had arrived in the country at the outset of the twentieth century. He praised the governments of the 1880s, under which he had embarked on his course as a pioneer. And although he set apart president Alvear (1922-28), he criticized the *Radicales*[2] for their scant capacity for action, from Irigoyen (1916-22) to Illia (1963-66). His opinion was that *Radicales* always acted contrary to the Roman dictum "Res, non verba" (things, not words) which he used as the family motto.

But he was most critical of Perón, whom he called a liar, an irresponsible demagogue, a thief, a man devoid of ethics and responsible for the immense slump that the country fell into under his rule.

Don Santiago charged Perón with the moral degradation that in his view the dictator had fostered in the population, which was taught to think about nothing but its own rights, forgetting about its duties. Neither did he excuse Perón for his Fascist methods, his opportunism at declaring war on Germany after this nation had been defeated, with the sole purpose of taking possession of German companies in Argentina. A complete citizen like don Santiago could not admit the personality cult promoted by Perón and Evita, and neither the perks and immunity before the law which the friends of the

---

[2] Radicales: Members of the middle-of-the-road Unión Cívica Radical political party, founded towards the end of the Nineteenth century and which concentrated the opposition to Perón during the latter's mandate (1946-55; 1973-76).

regime enjoyed, or the unconditional and corrupt alliances with the trade unions.

One day in September, 1955, my father had taken me on a trip to Zapala, in Río Negro, in the old Dodge station wagon the family owned then. I was five. We left at six in the morning on a very cold day, with a thick fog covering valleys and mountains. On arrival at the military barracks in Junín de los Andes we ran into a roadblock set up on a curve. After waiting for a while in the car, still before sunrise and bitterly cold, the officer who commanded the guard recognized my father, and said a few words which shocked me so much that I still remember them: "Don Andrés, go back to the estancia and stay there, otherwise I'll have to take you inside immediately".

We returned and spent the rest of the day listening to the communiqués of an insurrection, afraid that Perón would manage to stifle the uprising, because it was rumored that if they won, the Peronists would take possession of all property and distribute it among their friends. When Perón finally boarded a Paraguayan gunboat that took him into exile, my grandfather uncorked one of the few Pommery champagne bottles he kept in the wine cellar and a joyous celebration followed.

Even leaving aside his grudge against Peronism, my grandfather had no respect for the Argentine political breed which, in his last letter to his brother José, written in September 1970, he described with conviction as infamous. His criticism focused on the politicians' incompetence in addressing the real problems that appeared, their propensity to lie to the people, their lack of commitment to the public weal, and their dishonesty.

For a convinced humanist as he was, that a person in government should hide facts from those governed by lying was an insult to the intellectual capacity of any human being.

When in 1957 my father was elected representative to the convention that would draft the constitution for the province of Neuquén, my grandfather had his doubts about this decision, but finally the tradition of the Larminat family of serving the State prevailed, and he gave his approval. My mother on the other hand, disliked this job my father had undertaken, and found his absence hard to bear, because at that time the city of Neuquén, where the Constituent Convention held its sessions, was inadequately communicated with our area, and my father spent many weeks away. Even so it was a period of learning and of achievements, and it was then that my father befriended don Felipe Sapag, who would become the most important man of political action in the province.

Don Santiago's line in politics was by no means regressive, and bore a genuine sensitivity towards contemporary problems. When the events of May 1968 took place in France, he wrote to his brothers, who lived in fear of the disturbances, that he thought it was natural for youth to rebel against a society that had cooped them up in limited functions, without any room for fantasy, for individual preferences or for free will. He said in a letter "these poor youths are subject to the same treatment we deal the sheep in Patagonia to bathe them: we round them up in smaller and smaller corrals, and in the end we put them in a narrow gangway leading them to a tub into which they fall and almost drown every time. I think it is not only normal, but even desirable that these youths should try to jump the fence of the stupid corral before falling into the tub".

Don Santiago had a strong and authoritarian personality, which he concealed under the most perfect and immutable courtesy. Sometimes his anger would be volcanic, and would build up to a wrath of gigantic proportions, but he would never utter a single foul word. He could state his ideas using the most polished language and the most adequate and precise wording, and whenever he delivered an indication or an order there could be no misunderstanding whatsoever as to its meaning. He was a proud man, and held himself in high regard, a trait which sometimes led people to consider him supercilious. He also tended to get his own way in all matters, and at times he would relegate the rights and aspirations of other members of his family and his circle, as what he tought was important always had priority.

A patriarchal atmosphere ruled his home. In the sitting room, kept warm by an enameled cast iron salamander , there were many objects representing the *pater familias.* The decorations that he had been awarded during the war were kept in a wooden cabinet with glass doors. We children were fascinated by these decorations, attracted by the colored silk ribbons and the golden brilliance of the medals; he never allowed us to touch them. A framed photograph of the family house in Sologne hung on a wall, with some of his watercolors. There was also some paraphernalia from his travels in Northern Africa.

In the dining room, an enormous round table could sit about twenty. That room had wood paneling, and two large windows which opened onto the old tennis court; my grandmother's piano occupied one corner. Even less in agreement with the rest of the furniture, there was a large picture on a wall, an engraving with a scene from the Punic Wars showing Hannibal entering Italy with his elephants and killing Romans right and left. We were very fond of this engraving, for its violence and the elephants.

Food was simple and abundant, prepared with products from the estancia: chickens, eggs, butter, *chicha* (a very dry cider made with the small bitter apples from the estate orchards); meat, almost always lamb in summer and tough meat of old cows in winter. Desserts in summer were fruit, such as raspberry and red currant, or quince from the vegetable garden, and in winter a kind of vanilla cream with caramel called "bouillie blanche" (white pap) which we children adored. There was also delicious dry fruit prepared in a firewood drier kept in the upper floor of the house, which was filled with an extraordinary perfume when prunes, apples or pears from the orchard were being dried.

Towards the end of his life don Santiago did little work in the fields; the handling of livestock was left to his two sons. He only appeared in the corrals when the important springtime and fall jobs were being carried out, especially tasks involving sheep, which were the most impressive. He always kept in touch with the activities on the estancia, discussing with my father and my uncle the work the farmhands did, the results of parturition, the weight and quality of the wool... In my memory there is the comforting scene of the three of them engaged in conversation, amid thousands of sheep being sheared or driven through the anti-mange bath that was standard once or twice a year.

At that time my grandfather was more interested in the trees in his park than in his animals, and he spent considerable time walking and planting new species that he brought from his travels or were sent to him by friends. Sometimes we would find him deep inside a wood carrying his pruning handsaw, dressed in his usual beige cotton fatigues, opening paths (which he called "the circuit for walks"), or deciding on the construction of a small bridge over a stream, or installing a park bench here or there so that my grandmother, who was a great walker in the park, could sit and rest.

Don Santiago and his sheep

He had a small nursery garden in which he prepared his plants and sowed his seeds –different to and separate from the large one which served the *estancia*– that was a square of about one fourth of a hectare surrounded by a wire-netting fence to protect the seedlings from hares. His nursery garden had a small adobe cottage with a tin roof made from empty oil cans; we called it "the Panchatière" because once it had been inhabited by a woman by the name of Pancha.

My grandfather spent much time working in his nursery garden, and kept his tools in the cottage. This construction had two rooms where the hams were kept in great vats, old wine casks which had been cut in the middle and filled with brine.

A task which was particularly enjoyable, and in which the whole family took part in the month of June, was the quartering and dressing of slaughtered hogs. This job demanded several days, and the result were the hams, which were dipped in the vats after rubbing them with saltpeter and spices. They were smoked with a grass which abounds in the fields, dubbed by us "the ham's herb".

Don Santiago supervised everything, moving from one work group to the next, commenting on the taste and seasoning of each product. Apart from ham, the production included black and white blood sausages, pork cheese, paté de foie, salami, smoked sirloin, shoulder, and finally everything was stored in the Panchatière. Other vats in the cottage contained sauerkraut, made by my aunts in winter when cabbage was ripe. After washing the leaves with iced water, the cabbage was chopped with a sort of cutting railing placed on top of the vat, storing it in layers alternated with rock salt, laurel leaves and black juniper fruit that we harvested with my brothers and cousins, pricking our fingers.

There was also in the cottage a variety of fine-smelling fruit on the shelves, and eggs in vats with a fluid to preserve them, since at that time there was no refrigerator on the estancia. All this production was continued by my father for many more years.

Another job that attracted us children was the construction of wheels for the carts. At that time there were no good roads, and in the country everything had to be transported in very solid carts drawn by oxen, which were built for our estate by a Chilean called Villablanca, with whom I was on friendly terms. He was a hard-working, crabby man, an artist as a carpenter and as a blacksmith, and his hands produced carts from the first nail to the final coat of paint. He worked in a shed close to my grandfather's, naturally it was called the Blacksmith's. That was where the cart wheels were encased in iron rims once a year, a show never to be missed.

Villablanca worked for months preparing the boxes for the carts, then focusing on the wheels, which had a diameter of one meter sixty centimeters and were made of hardwood brought from the northern provinces. Made of wood were the hub, the spokes and the circumference in which the spokes were fitted. Two or three pairs were manufactured each year, and the process of fitting the rims onto the wooden wheels was sheer magic. These rims were long steel strips half an inch thick, which Villablanca shaped in the forge, until he achieved a circle with a diameter slightly smaller than that of the wheels. Then all hands would be summoned, and we children joined with glee. Huge fires were lit to make the rims red hot.

Villablanca's calculations were so precise that with the expansion produced by the heat the wheel tightly fitted the rim, the wood would begin to burn under the overheated iron. Immediately, buckets of cold water were poured on the newly armored wheel to adjust the rim to the wood which would have to withstand years of work ahead over the stones and rocks on the roads. My grandfather would also watch the show: sitting at a distance, drawing caricatures of the folk taking part.

Villablanca would sweat copiously, replacing the liquid lost with *chicha*, so that by the end of a job he was utterly drunk. The whole process was a celebration, which to us held elements of magic, with those enormous circular fires, from which a number of small men lifted a great, bright metal ring and rushed with it to the wheel, where a new fire sprang up in little flames from the wood.

Another annual event that congregated the whole family was the horse-taming. On the estancia there were two packs of about fifteen mares each, one with the draft stallion and the other with the thoroughbred.

Each year, there were twenty-five or thirty colts of all sizes and colors to be tamed, and that was an occasion that nobody wanted to miss. It was held in a special ring about five kilometers from the houses, the "Taming Corral", where there was a beautiful fountainhead that emerged from the slope of a mountain, a pine coppice, an apple orchard and a great round picket corral in which the colts were kept.

On the morning of the appointed day everybody showed up, from the tamer and his assistants to my grandfather, my grandmother, aunts, and the whole lot of us, including uncle Esteban, aunt Genoveva and the inhabitants on the north side of the river who arrived in their four-wheel drive jeep, then a technological wonder. We used to set up camp beside the natural spring, in a series of tiers made with the resources available, earth and grass, and where everybody carried their picnic, wicker baskets with all kinds of supplies: salamis, ham, bread, cider, fruit and cheese, in a Patagonian version of the Epsom Derby. The difference was that, if there wasn't a strong wind, a fire would be lit to heat the kettle and have some *maté* [3], and sometimes even a chunk of meat would be cooked.

The tamer and his assistants began work with each lassoing a colt. It was a complicated endeavor, because the animals had lived free in the fields since they were born and were completely wild. Some would let themselves be saddled, while others rolled on the ground and then bounded like devils. Sometimes the wind made matters

---

[3] Maté: An infusion of native indian origin made with a herb, yerba maté, sipped from a gourd with a small tube.

worse, sweeping the trappings off the colts' backs before the girths could be tightened.

Once all was ready the candidate would mount, whip in hand and well-spurred, and when he shouted "Let him go!" the colt leaped madly in curvets and then shoot off at full gallop. The tamer's "godfathers" accompanied him on a ride totally different to the horse-taming contests held in villages nowadays. The trio would literally get lost over the horizon, and quite often the horseman would end up thrown head first into a large thorny bush, from where he had to return on foot, while his "godfathers" tried to lasso the runaway colt and take it back to the corral.

My grandfather enjoyed this show very much, commenting on each gallop with the spectators, expressing his opinion to my father and my uncle Bernardo about the nature and mien of every colt.

His past as a cavalry officer during the Great War led him to think better of the heavy and sturdy horses rather than the emaciated thoroughbreds. When some interesting scene took place he would record it with his box-type 16 mm. spring-operated Kodak. That camera was a marvel of simplicity and efficiency. In the end my grandfather gave it to me, when he bought a new double eight format, which never worked as well as the Kodak. In those times the first Kodakchrome films were not developed in Argentina. We sent ours via air mail to France, and had them returned two months later, without a single one getting lost, ever. Their arrival offered a good opportunity to organize a gathering in the Old House, where we would all comment on the highlights of the taming.

The finest program for a Sunday was to go hare hunting. As from March and during all of the fall and winter, we went hunting hares in the valleys that surrounded the homestead.

Generally my grandfather would go, with my great-uncle Bernardo, my father and sometimes don Esteban too, when he came with his family to Sunday mass. The hunters were the adults, all of them carrying .12 caliber double-barrel shotguns and a belt full of cartridges. They were accompanied by some of the aunts and invariably by a bunch of kids. We took several dogs, and the technique consisted of walking in a line, the hunters intercalated with the non-hunters. The dogs came and went along the line picking up the hares. The closest hunter always had priority to shoot.

We children had to collect the hares and take them to the estancia, where for a few coins we skinned them. In winter the hides were sold and at a good price. In summer there was such an abundance of hares and the damage they inflicted upon the plantations of pines was so great, that we also went hunting just to bring a few for the kitchen. Mostly the dead were left in the fields, only their ears cut to keep count.

The takings were abundant, and sometimes we got as many as sixty pieces in one single morning, which made a heavy burden for our cousins and ourselves to get home. It was a splendid program which I was very fond of. We departed on those winter mornings with nature in deep silence, with scarcely a breeze, the ground covered in frost, the branches with a white topping, and only the low purring of the river for sound. The landscape bore a gray and beige hue, with a few touches of orange on the willow trunks and the reflection of the sky on the lagoons. We used to hike for several hours against the wind, and at a certain time we returned to the road to meet my mother, who came to our rescue in the car. That was a blessing, because we were tired of hiking with a load of hares on our backs. Sometimes, when the load was plentiful, we would stop and skin the hares at speed, and naturally there would be races to determine who was the fastest and who caused the least damage to the hides. Often my grandfather would produce his watercolors and paint some scene.

Don Santiago had a passion for drawing and painting that he kept throughout his life. Anywhere he was he would produce a notebook, his pencils or watercolors, and produce well crafted caricatures or sketches, of trees or animals. Sometimes he showed us the drawings that were the result of his travels, which he went on regularly, either when he returned to France, or when he went to Morocco, or, within Argentina, to Salta and Jujuy, two provinces whose austere and colorful landscapes he admired.

By family request, he had begun to tell his life in watercolors, showing in pictures the events that accompanied his settling in Argentina and the early years of the estancia. He was not able to complete his story, but he produced a good number of pictures, which he photographed and turned into slides that were screened at family gatherings. We also witnessed the slides made from his snapshots of nature; he was a photography enthusiast and kept pictures since he first arrived in the country. On one occasion, about 1909, he was engaged by the police commissioner in Chimpay to photograph the body of a gaucho who had been murdered in the local *pulpería*[4].

However, the program that excited us children most was the screening, in the big hall of the Old House, of the films he had made in 16 mm. throughout his life; my father and his brother and sisters when young, the work on the *estancia*, the French cousins, and sometimes even ourselves. Don Santiago used to accompany these sessions with his comments, historical, political and sociological, while everyone in the family joined in voicing his or her opinion upon whatever was shown on the screen.

There was only one film that had been bought, very popular among us kids, which was not frequently shown so that we didn't lose interest. It was a Felix the Cat cartoon, in black and white, which nowadays would seem insignificant, but which for us was an opening into a world we ignored completely, because we had no access to cartoons. Needless to say there was no television and we never went to the cinema, which was in town, too far away, doubly ignored because we had no means of knowing what they were showing.

[4] Pulpería: The general store in the country, selling goods and liquor, where gauchos and farmhands gathered.

Don Santiago with his sons Andrés and Bernardo

Don Santiago with his wife Doña Magdalena

My grandfather believed that life had been degraded to a great extent by bureaucracy and the gradual obliteration of trust, which forced him to put things in writing in excess. He said, commenting on the administration work carried out by his sons, that "there is no longer any time to stop and reflect, or to foresee and prevent. This is no life, compared to the private, peaceful, productive and much less superficial life we led before".

Don Santiago also had a flair for construction. He believed that every human being had to leave some concrete testimony of his brief residence in this world, and he had chosen to leave a large family and an important settlement at *Cerro de los Pinos*, Pine Trees Mount. Among other projects, he had made the promise together with my grandmother that he would build a chapel to thank the Virgin for the safe return of their two sons from the war. I chanced to follow the planning and construction of this chapel. I remember, as a small child, the conversations about the plans, the sketches that my grandfather brought from France and which were discussed with don David Marré, the constructor who had made all the important buildings on the *estancia*. Don David was an Italian immigrant who had settled in San Martín de los Andes, a self-taught man who had started as a mason, finally becoming a master builder. The fact that my grandfather entrusted him with the construction of the chapel filled him with pride, as building a temple is a landmark in the life of any builder, and more so if he is Italian.

The foundations were drawn in the tract of land that lay in front of our houses, and from that moment on don Santiago followed the progress daily, as the walls began to gain height, stone by stone. The day arrived when the crowning point of the building had to be installed. It was the carved stone vault under which the altar would be located. My grandfather had told me that it was then when it would be known if Marré was really capable of building a church: the key moment would be when the scaffolding upon which the vault stones rested was withdrawn, while the pointing was left to harden.

The Chapel at Pines Mount

That day, in the spring of 1956, Marré arrived very early, while all of us showed up later to witness the moment of truth. In his imperfect Spanish, turned into even more of a jargon than ever because of his nervousness, he ordered his masons to remove the props that supported the stones. With each prop that was removed we held our breath, us kids secretly hoping that everything would collapse. But when the last stanchion was taken away and it was seen that there was no tumbling of the building, the grownups clapped and congratulated Marré, then going over to my grandfather's to celebrate with a cup of wine, while we children left the site thoroughly disappointed.

To complete the chapel don Santiago engaged a French sculptor from Bretagne to make a Way of the Cross, which arrived some years later in an enormous wooden box, the largest we had ever seen. My grandfather, very proud of his purchase, opened the box and hung the fifteen terra cotta stations in the chapel, a duty he undertook aided by my grandmother and my aunts.

In February 1962, the newly-appointed bishop for the province of Neuquén, Jaime de Nevares, came to bless the chapel, which led to a very good relationship with my grandfather. They had a brief dialogue in Latin, to everyone's admiration. Later the acquaintance with Monsignor de Nevares became strained due to political differences, as the bishop's convictions were seen to move towards an increasingly intransigent left.

Once the chapel was inaugurated my grandparents regularly invited a priest with whom they were on friendly terms to stay in their home during summer. We children used to act as altar boys at the daily mass. These priests were as a rule very special, many of them erudite scholars, or travelers, and invariably most interesting. One of them was a Russian by the name of Alexander Kulik, a priest with the Russian Coptic Church and a true philosopher. He taught me to play chess, a game at which he was on a par with professional masters. He also sang beautifully, with a typically Russian deep bass voice; his participation produced a remarkable upgrading of the chapel singing. After mass, as soon as he returned from the vestry, he would join the choir, softly at first, and then with greater volume until his voice drowned all others. He was fond of sitting under the weeping willow at the entrance to my grandfather's house, having a glass of cold *chicha* and talking about the world, about religion or politics. Father Alexander finally went to Italy to a position in the Vatican, and we saw him no more.

Another remarkable priest was Juan Dan, a very affectionate Rumanian priest who for many years spent a month in summer at my grandparents'. At first he had to face the challenge of substituting Father Alexander, none too easy because we all missed the Russian very much. But he also managed to earn our affection, feeling likewise towards us. He was a parish priest with his national community in Buenos Aires, and professor of Canonical Law at the Salvador University, and ended up loving us as though we were his own family, which had remained in Rumania under the cruel Ceaucescu regime. He baptized several of my cousins, and much later my daughter Victoria. He was fond of fishing trout, considering them his personal enemies. He returned each year ready for his hand-to-hand battles with the fish, never accepting to return any alive to the river: if he caught them, he had a right to eat them.

In 1992 I went to school in Buenos Aires, as my parents decided to send me to the "Collège Français de Buenos Aires", and contact with my grandfather became less frequent, but we corresponded regularly, and saw each other during my holidays. Don Santiago had always time and was interested in talking with me about my studies and my projects. When he came to Buenos Aires in winter, our favorite program –my cousin María Ana's and mine– was to be invited to the Ideal tea room on Suipacha street, where in the afternoon an orchestra played in the balcony on the first floor. My grandfather treated us to hot chocolate, so thick that the spoon would stand upright in the cup, and there we talked about the future, about politics, our studies and about the films that were being shown in the city, since he loved going to the cinema.

When I decided to study engineering he recommended the Sainte Geneviève School to me, an institute in Versailles (France) run by the Company of Jesus and specializing in the preparatory courses for the great French engineering schools, such as the École Polytéchnique and the École Centrale. Several members of the family in the last two centuries, among them his own father, had attended them. On a trip he made to France about that time he went to the school to learn about registration requirements, then encouraged me to try for entrance, although it was a tough proposal. I felt that if I did study in France it would be difficult for me to resettle in Argentina upon return, and I wanted to live here, so I decided to apply at the University of Buenos Aires. This was a very different option but with exciting prospects, both from an academic angle which was extremely satisfactory, and as a life experience, because it turned out to be an unforgettable period of political activism and of transformations in Argentine society.

When I was in my third year, in October 1970, my grandfather fell ill, and died within a few days, on the 10th. Up to the last moment he kept all his wits about him.

At the *estancia*, in the family, in my feelings, there was a great vacuum. He lies in the small cemetery of *Cerro de los Pinos*, under a cypress which he had planted. Now his tomb is accompanied bythat of my grandmother, who loved him so much and always stood by him. The site is marked by two wooden crosses painted white.

For his great influence on my learning, for the importance he had in my first rational look at life and mankind, don Santiago occupies a privileged place in my memories.

In this book I shall try to describe his life, and discuss the reasons that brought him to Patagonia. It will be seen that only a person with an extremely ambitious and daring personality could have embarked with his family on such an exotic adventure. My grandfather was blessed with an encyclopedic culture, and he could rely on a family project in agreement with his own father and his brothers, a true long-term endeavor with a strategy of development.

I have been lucky to have had access to documents, such as old letters, watercolors and period photographs, particularly a copy of his splendid war memoirs, with his watercolors, snapshots and exciting stories. I was also able to make use of the narrations of a number of persons who knew him, and who aided me in reconstructing the stories and legends that had marked my childhood.

My grandfather's adventure unfolds in the pages that follow.

Santiago de Larminat with his brother Etienne at Cerro de los Pinos in 1967

The Ancestors

Photograph of Thionville, late XIXth century

Y FAMILY ORIGINATED, AS FAR AS IT is known, in the French city of Thionville, close to the Luxembourg border. The first Larminat of whom we have information was an officer with the Imperial Army defending that township when the Condé clan tried to take possession of it, in 1643. Louis de Larminat, as he was called, was then a cadet. Some years later he joined the French forces as captain of the Royal Piemonte Regiment, a corps which under prince Condé de Coligny took part in the battle of St. Gothard, when the Turks were repelled before Vienna, in their advance over Europe.

It is not known where this Larminat came from. The name has an obvious French origin. Larminat, Larmignat, are surely deformations of the Armagnac party, the followers of Joan of Arc who in the XVth. Century opposed the Burgundians, their mortal enemies. During the Hundred Years' war the Armagnacs defended French legitimacy against the Burgundians, who had allied with a foreign dynasty.

The fact is that almost all these Larminats from the times of the monarchy (the Ancien Régime, as the French call it) were government officials: military officers, war commissioners, mayors, and they seem to have felt very comfortable in those positions. Many were the Larminats who abandoned activities which were better rewarded or of a higher standing to join the State, contributing their intelligence, their imagination and their enterprising spirit to serve the public interest. However, in the case of my grandfather, in spite of that background, he never attempted to obtain a public position, and, on the contrary, remained carefully at a distance from State officials throughout his life.

The Larminats served the State during more than three centuries, some of them risking their lives, as with a Jean de Larminat, mayor of Thionville, who in 1709 died of cold returning from Versailles, where he had gone to ask for aid for his town which had been isolated due to a severe winter. A less extreme service was the one rendered by Marie de Larminat, favorite lady-in-waiting to Empress Eugénie, during the last period of her reign and her exile. Marie was a beautiful, intelligent and congenial woman; she left a remarkable autobiography of her years with the emperors. She was not the only Larminat to leave France a valuable legacy. There was the splendid pine woods planted by Jean-Charles-Nicholas de Larminat in the previously sterile soil of Fontainebleau; the Pont Marie, one of the most becoming of Parisian bridges, constructed by a Marrier de Boisdhyver, a relative of the family; and the numerous military men who fell in action over three centuries in the defense of France. Jean de Larminat, who was my grandfather's father, was a driving force in the development of the railway system in France. This Jean was a son of Pierre-Louis-Edouard, the child of Jean-Charles-Nicholas, a great developer of forestry.

To begin with the last mentioned, Jean-Charles-Nicholas de Larminat (1777-1840) was keeper of the Fontainebleau Forests Preserver, being granted the title of baron for his services; he dealt very closely with the king, and with his wife Victorine Marrier de Boisdhyver constituted an elegant, affable and well-known couple in Fontainebleau. There is an anecdote which has been proudly kept in the family. One day, seeing Jean-Charles-Nicholas enter the court with his wife on his arm, king Charles X exclaimed: "Look, the most beautiful couple in France has just entered the palace of Versailles".

Jean-Charles-Nicholas dedicated his life to the improvement of the royal forests, and to this day the avenues which he designed and planted in Fontainebleau may be walked, and they bear names that honor his spirit, such as the avenues Friendship, Nobility and Two Sisters, and obviously the Larminat avenue, which runs in front of the house that was his. He succeeded in reproducing certain varieties of resinous pines with which he was able to populate barren and desolate lands, and even today his achievements are mentioned in specialist works. With a spirit that my grandfather inherited, Jean-Charles-Nicholas escaped routine; he was a traveler, he learned from the men he met, and he developed his own ideas from reflection and observation.

His son Pierre-Louis-Edouard (1811-1895) could not follow in his father's footsteps for health reasons, but had a great love for nature, which he communicated to his fourteen children in his large home in Beaurieux, in the Soissonais region. This is an area of great beauty located as an extension of Ile de France towards the l'Aisne valleys that rise to the naked plains of Champagne. The so French atmosphere of La Fontaine's fables, between rustic and refined, reigned there; Chateau Thierry was not far, and the family spirit was imbued with the poetry of fields and woods. Edouard loved nature, as can be ascertained by the collection of butterflies, insects, plants and fossils that he left.

His son Jean, my great-grandfather (1855-1929) enjoyed a polished education. For his secondary tuition he attended Saint-Clément School, in Metz, where he rubbed shoulders with several among the offspring of Central European families that later played important scientific and political roles, such as Auguste Potocki, count Bethlen and count Michael of Braganza. He continued his studies in the famed École Polythechnique, where he formed part of a brilliant and inseparable trio with the future marshal Lyautey and with Antonin de Margerie. First as a student, then as a graduate engineer, Jean mingled with the rank and fashion and discussed the novelties that electricity and oil were in those times. The blueprints for mass industrial production were being devised, and there was also talk about strikes, which were becoming increasingly frequent. He also witnessed the bloody fighting during the Paris Commune, as well as the development of industrial growth. As the end of the century approached, Europe was changing with accelerated rhythm; there were experiments with plastics, and the telephone was being improved. While the Parisian streets were furnished with electric lighting, Jean became interested in photography, a passion which his children would inherit, and he was captivated by the arrival of cinema, considered by many as having no future.

On November 29, 1881, Jean married Marguerite Colas des Francs in Orléans. Marguerite belonged on her father Arthur's side to an old family settled near the city. This family was large and united by strong bonds. On the side of her mother, Ambroise-Blanche-Marie Lockhart, she was part of a Scottish family with a historical background, as an anecdote shows. "In the year of Our Lord 1330, the Scottish laird Sir James Douglas started on a long journey with his squire Simon Lockhart to comply with the last will of the king of Scotland Robert Bruce; the king had been a crusader and he wanted his heart to be carried to the Holy Land. Sir James was accompanied by a full entourage to protect him and assist him on his mission. He was carrying the king's heart in a gold locket fastened to a lanyard. They boarded ship in Glasgow and sailed to Bilbao with the intention of crossing the Iberian peninsula and embarking again to sail the Mediterranean and so reach Palestine. However, upon arriving in Spain, the travelers were invited by Alphonse XI, king of Castile and Leon, to accompany him in a battle against the Moors in which he was about to engage. This battle turned out to be terrible; most of the Scotsmen died, among them Douglas.

"Simon Lockhart heroically retrieved the locket that Douglas carried, and in the face of disaster decided to abandon the mission and return with the relic to Scotland. In agreement with the Scottish royal family he deposited his king's heart at Melrose Abbey, and as a reminder of the epic he included in his coat of arms a heart surrounded by a chain, fastened by an open padlock. To this he added the graceful motto: *Corda serrata pando*, which means 'I open the locked hearts'."

A branch of the Lockharts emigrated to Argentina, renewing in this country the close relationship that existed with the Larminats.

My great-grandfather had eight children with Marguerite. She died suddenly in 1896. A few years before, in 1891, Jean had bought a large hunting lodge which he called "La Hardonnière" in Chambord, an area of splendid forests that encircle one of the most famous castles in the Loire valley. The whole region is under the influence of that castle, which was built by Francis I at the outset of the XVI century according to plans drafted by Leonardo da Vinci. It is surrounded by forests that are a reserve of wild boar, deer and birds. The 100 hectares of land bought by Jean de Larminat were in this beautiful environment.

He had not been originally a farming man. On the contrary, he had a flair for engineering and was knowledgeable in the construction of transport infrastructures. The time for air transportation had not yet arrived. This means of conveying goods was as a rule only promoted in futuristic books such as those of Jules Verne, so throughout Europe enormous investments were being poured into improvement of land transportation.

Jean's zeal for the technical marvels of those years led him to be a protagonist in the development of an element of fundamental importance in the growth of Europe and the whole world: the railroad. When he was thirty he joined the West Railway Company of France as an engineer becoming General Director after a brilliant career, at scarcely forty-four.

The *Le Figaro* newspaper interviewed him extensively on the day he was appointed for this job, on November 24, 1899. Three years later Jean resigned, when Clémenceau organized the take over of the railways by the State. After that, the duration of his stays at La Hardonnière became longer; never, not even in the moments of the most intense professional and social activity, had he been absent from this beautiful estate, a harbor of peace for his large family. With time, following the family tradition, he became fully attached to the soil and its blessing, and developed a special interest in forests and pine trees.

Five years after losing his wife, Jean married again, this time a neighbor from the region of Sologne, Régine Aubépin de Lamothe-Dreuzy, with whom he had six more children, thus making five daughters and nine sons between his two marriages. The prolific tradition of the family has hardly ever been neglected.

When my grandfather was asked about his family's laurels his answer was rather modest: "Our titles of nobility are not so many to give cause for vanity; we are not nobles of the land, we have not been prominent gentlemen of either nobility or arms, although many of us have served as officers in the king's armies, in the emperor's and in those of the Republic. We belong to the small provincial nobility that earned its titles from its functions or positions serving the monarchy. But the consistency shown by the family, after three hundred years of honorably serving the State, the consistency of its alliances with families of the same social rank, often improving its position through marriage, has established a solid tradition of great education, of honor and generosity that holds its value; the full knowledge of the fount which is our source contributes to appreciate and maintain this tradition, in a century in which all values are being challenged".

The Decision: Why Argentina?

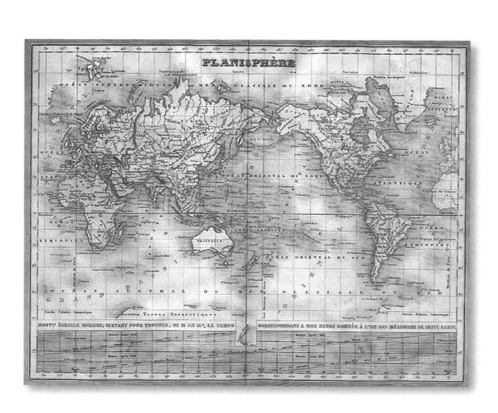

$\mathcal{M}$Y GRANDFATHER, JACQUES DE LARMINAT, was born on March 10, 1889. His childhood was spent in a religious, closely knit and socially active home. While his father made progress in his managerial career in the railway company, setting up their new home on the Avenue Bugeaud in Paris, his mother, Marguerite Colas des Francs, took care of their numerous children –Jacques was the fifth child and the fourth male– giving them an early formation both affectionate and austere, based on the principles of a well-known Catholic liberal educator of the nineteenth century, Monsignor Dupanloup. These principles were in tune with the clergyman's background; he had been bishop of the Orléans diocese, close to La Hardonnière, for almost three decades. Dupanloup was an active defender of private education and of the pursuit of excellence in all daily activities, having been a legislator, a member of the French Academy and restorer of the cult of Joan of Arc, which accounts for the great respect our family always held for this saint. Jacques received a shattering blow at the age of seven, when his mother died. His older sister Elizabeth took a leading role in the management of the family.

Jacques continued to receive the meticulous education that his father considered necessary. He completed his secondary studies at the well know Parisian school Gerson, and he traveled. At fifteen he spent some time in London with one of his brothers to polish his English, and from there visited Spain, Morocco, and naturally Germany, the powerful and threatening nation. Then under Kaiser Wilhelm I and chancellor Bismarck, Germany was experiencing a formidable industrial boom, had a solid economy and the best universities in the world. Later, Jacques won a place at the Paris Agronomy Institute, an establishment which issued degrees in farming engineering. Summers he spent at La Hardonnière.

The spread of colonialism was the backdrop to Jacques' childhood and early youth. The European powers competed to appropriate the largest share of the world. The Berlin Conference of 1884-5 divided and ruled Africa according to the interests of the different metropolis. No European nation was respectable if it lacked colonies to take them the European culture and civilization and from where the maximum commercial benefit could be extracted. No other culture existed aside from the one originated in Europe, and neither was there any place on earth that did not depend in one way or another on the European economy. That was the source of industrial manufactures and the destination of the raw materials that the colonial possessions yielded, and which Europe avidly consumed.

Newspapers focused on the events in the colonies, promoting interest in people who dreamed about becoming landowners, the owners of fertile land, where an open road for enterprise and work existed. That is how whole families were encouraged to try their luck in places as exotic as the Antilles, Morocco and Indochina.

When did this idea find its way into the Larminat family? What powerful lure drew some of its members to abandon the comfortable life of the Parisian high bourgeoisie, and embark on an uncertain adventure? There is no doubt that Jean, my grandfather's father, was the instigator of a family enterprise outside Europe.

From his position as director of a railway company he could see better than others the momentous progress and the tremendous difficulties that darkened the skies of the future. The head of a large family, he worried about the prospects for his children, and so began to consider creating a family branch in a remote and virgin site, where a project in accordance with his philosophy could be carried out: to leave a useful record of one's passing through the world.

Family documents show that his children were still small when possible destinations were discussed. Morocco, Nicaragua, the Antilles... Morocco was set aside; although marshal Lyautey, Jean's great friend and schoolmate was there, the character of the natives and the harsh environment did not attract him. Nicaragua was tempting, but its tropical climate, which meant fevers and strange illnesses, ran counter to the family tradition of manifold offspring. The Antilles were rejected for various reasons. How did the name of Argentina come up?

In truth, the selection was not left to chance. To begin with, Jean must have known that important French railway companies had invested in Argentina. In the last stages of the nineteenth century French financiers consolidated the presence of capital in the River Plate, to compete with British investments, which were then dominant. Between 1900 and 1914 there was a considerable flow of French investment to Latin America, but mainly to Argentina, where a substantial French community had settled. Cash flowed into the sugar and tannin industries, into banks and commercial establishments, and above all into mortgage debentures. This offensive was directed by the three most powerful investment banks in France: the Banque de l'Union Parisienne, the Banque de Paris et des Pays Bas, and the Banque de Crédit Mobilier. Their directors, who managed industrial and railway companies, became interested in the Argentine grain exports business. This prompted them to favor the laying of railway lines in cereal-growing regions, to run across the richest provinces and connect with the ports whence the produce was shipped to the world. The French railway companies were closely connected with some industrial and commercial corporations, such as La Forestal, the main producer of *quebracho*[5] wood and tannin; Louis Dreyfus and Bunge & Born, which operated in cereals, and the sugar refinery owned by Monsieur Hileret.

The combination of these formed a network of interests with great influence in the economies of the provinces of Chaco and Santa Fe, and overall the north of the country.

The railway lines which connected La Plata with Rosario (with an extension to General Villegas); the line connecting the port of Rosario, in the province of Santa Fe, with Resistencia, capital of Chaco province, and the important track joining the ports of Rosario and Puerto Belgrano, just out of the city of Bahia Blanca, are evidence of the interest that French financiers had burgeoning cereal business.

For these reasons, end-of-the-century Argentina was a topic of conversation in France and all Europe. In the World Fair held in Paris in 1889, the year my grandfather was born, Argentina erected a 1,600 square meters pavilion behind the Eiffel tower (where work was just commencing).

This pavilion was meant to show the opulence of the young nation. It had an iron structure (constructed by architect Ballu, with a generous provision of cast iron ornaments, moldings and sculptures for which the best French artists were engaged), and exhibited the country's raw materials: cereal, wood, hide, marble, wool, wine and particularly a novel-technology cold-storage chamber.

For its inauguration, on May 25, 1889, the pavilion was lit by hundreds of electric bulbs, which were also new at that time, whose light was colored by green, blue, royal purple and red colors, while all exteriors were covered with multicolored glass fragments, resembling diamond tips.

[5] Quebracho: From the Spanish *quiebrahacha*, literally ax breaker, because of the hardness of its wood.

The Paris Pavilion reerected in Plaza San Martín in 1910

The French president Sadi Carnot attended the ceremony, and so did Carlos Pellegrini, the Argentine vice-president. (This pavilion was later re-erected on Plaza San Martín in Buenos Aires to house the Fine Arts Exhibition during the Centenary celebrations, in 1910).

The chronicles of those times devoted considerable space to Argentine travelers and diplomats in Paris. It is through these accounts that we know that Mariano Balcarce, who became ambassador in Paris in the 1880s, was connected with the top echelons of society in the Second Empire, due to the influence of his father in law, José de San Martín, to his own personal abilities, and also to his close relationship with the bankers Aguado, who were on intimate terms with Napoleon III. He was by no means the sole prominent Argentine to be talked about in Paris at that time. Powered by their income, many *estancieros*[6] lived amid luxury and pomposity in the French capital, where they settled for long periods. The expression *"riche comme un argentin"*, rich as an Argentine, became almost a proverb. In some cases it gave rise to mockery and disdain, due to the purse-proud parvenus who only had the excess of money behind them, but in many other cases they were cultured and refined men and women, who visited museums and contacted artists and men of letters.

The testimonies left by the talented members of the 1880s generation, Eduardo Wilde, Lucio V. López, Miguel Cané, show that these Argentines went to Paris as to "the new Athens" (as Cané calls it in his book *En Viaje*, Traveling) to complete their education and to imbibe the models of culture that they wanted to set up in their homeland. Among the writers who looked for the direction of the new sensitivities in the cosmopolitan atmosphere of the French capital were Leopoldo Lugones, Ricardo Güiraldes and Oliverio Girondo. As for the artists, these included Rogelio Yrurtia, Eduardo Sívori, Lucio Correa Morales, Emilio Pettoruti, Antonio Berni and Lino Eneas Spilimbergo.

Some ladies from Argentine high society had literary salons in Paris. Among them were Sara Wilkinson Santamarina, and Regina Pacini de Alvear, who welcomed her guests at her Coeur Volant mansion, and Susana Torres Castex, who did likewise in the salons of the Plaza-Athénée Hotel, and María Luisa Dose Larivière (who in 1946 held dinners attended by De Gaulle and Mendes-France). Widely differing characters could be seen at these gatherings, such as the politician Georges Clémençeau, general Foch, the writers Jules Supervielle and Romain Rolland, and the critics Pierre Paul Plan and Charles Maurice. Coming from an almost provincial society, the Argentines in Paris honed their personalities and became refined, leaving in France an impression of great distinction. Some of them bought works of art that can be seen today in Argentine museums, such as the Santamarina, Hirsch and Bemberg collections.

[6] Estancieros: Important farmer in Argentina.

For others, Paris was an opportunity to squander; the unstinted marginal profit that the possession of land yielded in those times allowed lives of idleness and ostentation, in the city that Argentines had always seen as the capital of the world. The many years spent there by Federico de Alvear with his family, recalled by his daughter Felisa Alvear de Santa Coloma, are a clear example of the lifestyle of the big *estancieros* in Paris: while her mother went from one antique shop to another, buying precious furniture, the daughters studied design at the Julien Academy, and the father went to the horse races at Longchamps and Chantilly. The family had three automobiles, and the numerous staff in domestic service wore livery with the initials "F de A" stamped on the buttons. (In 1926, when he returned to Argentina, Alvear had to mortgage all his estate at a loss. He was unable to keep his magnificent residence on the corner of Libertador Avenue and Billinghurst street, today the site of the Italian embassy.) Another dashing and elegant millionaire was Aarón de Anchorena, the Honorary Secretary of the Argentine Legation in Paris between 1902 and 1916. A permanent feature in the social columns of the time, photographs show him in the Bois de Boulogne displaying the breed of his horses and the beauty of the ladies in his entourage. His parties, which he gave aboard his yacht *Pampa*, anchored in the Cote d'Azur, were famous.

Around 1902 tango became the fashion in Paris. First with Alfredo Gobbi, later with Angel Villoldo, the Argentine dance music was the boom of the pre-war salons in Paris. The Buenos Aires magazine *P.B.T.* titled an article in 1913 "Tangomania in Paris", which read: "Tango, in spite of moral considerations and the opinion of dancers of good taste, has become a real obsession in Paris", adding that personalities such as the heir don Luis de Orléans and the princess who was heiress to the Romanian throne paid large sums to learn to dance tango, in the arms of doubtful "professors" who had arrived from the river Plate.

By 1910 the Argentine community in Paris had become so numerous that it supported its own magazine, *Gustos y Gestos* (Tastes and Gestures), a posh fortnightly publication that established esthetic styles, communicated the indispensable information so as not to appear to be a *nouveau riche*, and while reporting on the parties that were thrown almost every day of the year, delivered a considerable amount of gossip. The Buenos Aires newspaper *La Prensa*, published its own edition on Paris.

All in all, Argentina was on the front page of French papers; curiosity for that remote and rich country had been aroused, and emigration did not appear to be a rash adventure. Books praising Argentina had already appeared in France, from Émile Daireaux's classic *Vie et moeurs à La Plata* (Life and Customs of La Plata[7]), published in Paris in 1888, two enormous volumes which were a form of guide for foreign companies looking to open in Argentina, to a book which appeared in 1906, clearly intended as publicity, *L'Argentine au Vingtième Siècle* (Argentina in the Twentieth Century), signed by A. Martínez and M. Lewandowsky, with an introduction by Carlos Pellegrini. This book communicated enthusiastically and with good arguments the financial advantages that the country offered to European investment. Another book from that time, *La République Argentine –Description, Étude Social et Historique*, by H.D. Sisson, predicted that Argentina would become "the Latin pole of America" and supported the claim with fifteen years' experience on the subject.

For Europe, Argentina was a curiosity and exotic, but also kindled hopes of wellbeing, in the case of the poor, and a suitable field to develop business, for the rich. My great-grandfather could not fail to feel attracted by the enormous, unimaginable extensions, the uniform plains, desert and fertile, christened the *Pampas*, and the cosmopolitan city with the romantic name of Buenos Aires, obstinately trying

---

[7] La Plata does not refer here to the city by that name, but is used by the author, as was common among writers and journalists, to designate the land which lay on the river Plate.

to look like Paris. Furthermore, the country was ruled by a refined high class that frittered away fortunes in their travels, a wealth that seemed to multiply by magic.

Almost fifty years before the Argentine adventure, a curious circumstance led to a more personal connection between my family and Argentina. Marie de Larminat was Empress Éugenie's lady-in-waiting, eventually to become her closest friend, and it is highly possible that Éugenie recalled for Marie her love story in Buenos Aires. In fact, Eugenia de Montijo, countess of Teba, had lived in the capital at the mouth of the river Plate, and had had Domingo de Arcos for fiancé. They were planning to marry, something which never happened due to a lack of the necessary funds to set up a home. Domingo's father was a millionaire, but he was on bad terms with his son and denied him all help. Eugenia's involvement with Argentines did not end there, because once back in Europe she developed a friendship with general Mansilla's family; it was he, as his writer son relates, the first to tell Eugenia, during a ball at the Tuilleries, that the future emperor Napoleon III, then an ambitious politician, had been observing her. Later general Mansilla became close to the emperors, a fact which makes it not improbable that he knew Marie de Larminat.

The fact remains that Argentina was the country chosen by the Larminats. In 1908 the family legally registered a civil partnership which they called "French Agricultural and Mining Company", securing the necessary capital to carry out the colonization project. Jacques decided to abandon his studies at the Institute Agronomique while in his last term, something almost nobody did at that advanced stage, but the challenge was worth it. In spite of his twenty years of age, he was endowed with an initiative and determination that earned him his father's trust, and so had the tremendous responsibility of being the first one to depart.

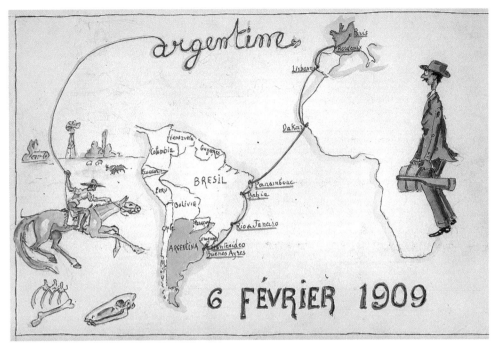

February 6, 1909. Jacques starts on his great adventure.

*February, 1909. After feeling the icy reception given his letters of introduction,
Jacques explores the city of Buenos Aires.*

May, 1909. Algarrobos: The windblows away the camp

March, 1909. Supper at the Chucul estancia, owned by Jean Guichard, in Algarrobos

1909. "La Mariquita", Córdoba. First round-up: "too many for comfort"

November, 1909. "La Pepa", the flooded pampa

December, 1909. Jacques takes photos of a murder at Chimpay, for the police.

1909. Piedra del Águila. Lamb roast with Bresler

The catcher caught. He who tries to fool another is fooled himself

August, 1910. Etienne, Jacques and André caught by the snow at Puente del Inca

August, 1910. Meeting in the Chilean forests: Kilaqueo, an Araucano from Pampa de Molco

Aout 1910 .- Le lac Lacar de Huahum à San Martin de los Andes
Plus de bateau !! La "canoa" des Salvavidas

August, 1910. On Lake Lácar from Huahum to San Martín de los Andes
in the canoe of the coastguards

10 Sept. 1910
COMME LE
SOIR tombait LE
CERRO APPARUT.

LE Chemin inondé

September 10, 1910. "Cerro de los Pinos", seen in the evening

*October, 1910. "La Avanzada". First round up of 4,000 sheep; 800 are missing,
stolen by Gregorio Pinuer who took them to Chile*

December 10, 1910. Arrival of the luggage that left Buenos Aires on July 31

1911. Estancia, staff

1911. First consignment: Payalef shuts in a herd

Taming: instant control

*1911. Don't make a noise. They forget a hard day's work
and the mangy sheep on their comfortable camp beds*

1911. First ascent to Cerro de los Pinos

Taming

1911. First gallop for Jacques, Etienne and André

1911. First crossing of the river Chimehuín

1911. Esteban marks the astronomical moon

1912. First harvest

February, 1912. River Senguerr

20 FÉVRIER 1912 · Filets et Rognons de Guanacs Font d'excellents Rotis; mais, un peu plus loin, entre le Rio Tucu Tucu et le Lac San Martin, pressés par la faim, nous mâchonmons les "Tientos" graisseux de l'Asador.

February 20, 1912. Guanaco sirloin and kidneys make delicious barbecues
Further on, hounded by hunger we chew the hide

CHASSE AUX BOLEADORES

CHOIQUES ÑAND

Catching young ñandú with bolas

December 6, 1913. Potrachoique (Chubut). The Tehuelche chief at one of the last camps breeds horses for flesh. We bought three as carriers

League 440. On learning of our arrival in Santa Cruz province, Juan de Liniers, Count of Buenos Aires, comes out to welcome us

The Great Adventure

LES MESSAGERIES MARITIMES

FONT LE TOUR DU MONDE

*Postcard of "Les Messageries Maritimes", the line
which took Don Santiago to Buenos Aires*

On February 6, 1909, Jacques de Larminat boarded a Messageries Maritimes ship, one of two French companies that sailed to South America. He began his journey in Bordeaux, with a farewell given by a beautiful snowstorm; a boat carried him to Ile Verte, where the *Cordillère* awaited him. The name, in the light of what followed, may be considered a premonition. Foul weather delayed departure, an inconvenience that cannot have troubled the young traveler, about to embark on his life's journey.

The *Cordillère* was a dazzling vessel. Carlos Pellegrini boarded it on his last trip to Europe, as he tried to restore his fragile health. These ships from French companies had an added attraction for Argentines, according to the great traveler Eduardo Mansilla: "Aboard French ships, the captain, always *charmant*, a real *homme du monde*, a man of the world, presides at his table, and when meals are over he offers his arm to the most important lady, and escorts her to the lounge. Travelers get to know the French officers; they ask about the most insignificant details of the journey, inquiring about everything; they investigate or they guess".

Normally the *Cordillère* took twenty days to complete the voyage, but this time it arrived in Buenos Aires on March 6. That was twenty-eight days after departure, having called at Lisbon, Dakkar, Pernambuco, Bahia, Rio de Janeiro and Montevideo. Jacques describes his impressions in his letters: Pernambuco's flying fish, the beauty of Bahía and Rio de Janeiro, the city surrounded by the cliffs known as *morros*, with their lavish vegetation... But he is astonished at not finding any of the trees he knows. There are no oaks, poplars, elms or chestnut trees; instead, there were arborescent bamboos, ferns and palm trees.

In the luxury transatlantic liners journeys were organized as a permanent party, with concerts arranged by passengers for the benefit of the emigrants who traveled in the lower decks, the celebrations on national days, costume parties when crossing the Equator, and dances every evening. For a twenty-year old youth it meant ceaseless mirth, but surely Jacques must not have forgotten that he was not on a pleasure trip but on the adventure of his life. He spent many hours contemplating the ever-changing scenery of the sea, a good companion of dreamers like himself, and tried to imagine the country towards which he was heading.

He had not boarded ship uninformed. Since the closing years of the nineteenth century the French press had been focusing assiduously on Argentina. A newspaper with a large circulation such as *Le Figaro* organized its foreign news in two sections: one dedicated to foreign countries in general, and the other to Latin America. The bulk of news referred to commerce and to politics when it could affect the former. A journalist from *Le Figaro*, Jules Huret, arrived in Argentina one year after Jacques, in time for the Centenary celebrations, held in 1910. He wrote a series of articles, later assembled in a book. Huret's conclusions are good proof of his optimism: "As far as political characteristics are concerned, those prevalent in Argentina are the same as in any other country undergoing the process of formation, and in certain aspects they resemble those of old and well-organized countries. The territory is enormous and very fertile. They have never used fertilizers. Stories are often heard about persons who arrived in Buenos Aires in dire poverty, becoming millionaires in ten years". This description coincides with the majority of the testimonies given by travelers who visited Argentina in the first two decades of the twentieth century: a new country, launched on a race to achieve fast and solid progress, with a future which could be no less than brilliant.

And that picture matched reality to perfection. Beginning in 1880 Argentina grew more, and at a faster pace, than any other country in the world. In the years immediately prior to Jacques' arrival, harvests had multiplied one hundred fold. French railways competed with the British, and the immigrants, the cattle and the sown fields expanded along territories gained at the expense of the native indians or the neighboring countries, or both at the same time.

Roca[8] had already conceded to Chile the Straits of Magellan, gaining the whole of Patagonia for Argentina. This immense extension had been claimed by Chile, but Roca took advantage of the war between Chile, Bolivia and Peru to trade Argentina's neutrality in exchange for that territory.

Britain, at that time still the leading nation in the world , having duplicated its investments in Mexico and Brazil, increased them five times in Argentina. Peace being assured in the country, all that was left was to work and make progress, and so it was. Prosperity brought changes in every respect. Big cities, like Buenos Aires and Rosario, were altered so much that in a few years they became unrecognizable. The Pampas ceased to be a sea of undergrowth that could be crisscrossed in all directions, and the new *estancias,* with their pastures, fences, windmills, alfalfa patches and their cereal-growing farms transformed the landscape.

---

[8] Julio Argentino Roca (1843-1914): An argentine general, twice President of the Republic, who secured Patagonia, opened it to colonization and settled the border problems with Chile.

The port of Buenos Aires in 1910

It was a prosperous and bustling period. Money circulated, production grew, services developed. Almost a million immigrants contributed new habits, traditions and ambitions. The economy was in order, and after the strain to settle the Baring Brothers loan, the services of the external debt were paid when they became due.

Within the field of public works there were splendid achievments. Engineer Eduardo Madero started the port of Buenos Aires; Puerto Belgrano was constructed in Bahía Blanca, and the main rivers in the country were dredged. Buenos Aires was becoming modern as fast as the European capitals; large buildings were erected, avenues were lit by gas, the telephone arrived, the best international shows included Buenos Aires as a destination, and exclusive clubs were being created, such as the Jockey Club and the French Club. A Botanical Garden and a Zoo which were models throughout America added an extra charm to the city.

Public education had prospered together with the economy, and the illiteracy index had diminished abruptly. Industrial and commercial schools were opened, as well as others directed at agriculture and the veterinary sciences. The Museum of Fine Arts was moved to a more suitable building, and the National Archive was created.

The Centenary celebrations had been in the works for several years; the country wanted to show the world that it had a history, and that it had attained a position among the powers. In that atmosphere of optimism, the fashionable words in books and newspapers were "future", "destiny", "greatness". And the great capital became embellished, adopting a style in which the French touch prevailed. Avenida de Mayo had been constructed as a Madrid look-alike, but in the northern part of the city, the palaces of the oligarchy resembled the most luxurious Parisian residences, and their owners, boasting their ability to spend, occupied these mansions only a few months or even weeks each year, because they spent most of the time in their no less luxurious mansions in the country, or in Paris. For the Centenary celebrations no expense was too much to inaugurate parks, to create promenades and gardens, to erect monuments, to renew public lighting and cobblestones...

However, perhaps due to the expectations that he had built in his imagination, Jacques felt disappointed upon arrival. He found Buenos Aires a sad city, even horrible. He thought he was witnessing the decoration of a great capital, but without a soul. Notwithstanding this, once he had settled, and as he began his rounds, the city seduced him. It was March, and the young *palos borrachos*[9] were in bloom, as were the jacarandas that Sarmiento had planted in Palermo to expel the ghost of Juan Manuel de Rosas[10].

---

[9] Literally drunken sticks, so called because the native Indians made use of the narcotic properties of its branches; cutting them up in small pieces and throwing them into a river, from where drowsy fish would rise to the surface.
[10] Dictator of Argentina, 1835-1852. Domingo F. Sarmiento was one of his most conspicuous opponents.

Although weighed down by the humid climate of the city, Jacques wanted to know it, and so walked it in all directions. He found the streets and sidewalks downtown too narrow, and also dangerous, as in some cases streetcars grazed the pedestrians. As work for the Centenary was in progress, part of the city was turned upside down, amid piles of rubble. The laying of the subway, the lighting of streets and avenues, the big theaters, the first automobiles, everything confirmed the impression that he had come to a city of endeavor and progress.

Love for trees, so ingrained in his family, prompted him to visit first and foremost the domain of one of the highly regarded Frenchmen in the city. He was Charles Thays, the director of Buenos Aires parks and plazas, and also the creator of the biggest and best private parks in the country. Thays visited the northern regions of Argentina, plus Bolivia and Brazil, looking for adequate species for Buenos Aires. He adapted some for their new destination, such as the *tipa*[11], which became a definitive feature of the city scenery.

Thays was the brain behind the Botanical Garden, the Palermo woods and, in the interior of the country, of Parque Independencia in Tucumán, a northern province where a large French colony resided. Jacques was bewildered by the Botanical Garden, where he found samples of flora from all over the world, plus a complete collection of Argentine trees, from the southernmost Antarctic beech, to carob trees, *quebrachos*, mahogany, cedars from the provinces of Tucumán and Mendoza and of course Thays' favorites, the *ombú*[12], the umbra tree, the *tipa*, and the *palo borracho*. And facing the Botanical Garden across the street, the Zoo, which Jacques visited and found very well supplied and maintained, thanks to the affectionate care given to it by its director, Clemente Onelli.

Together with trees, books were another of Jacques' passions.

[11] The *Tipuana tipu*, a yellow-flowered hardwood tree.
[12] The umbra tree, typical of the Pampas, not producing wood but reaching large proportions, useful for its shade.

Palermo at the start of the twentieth century

Among the letters of introduction he brought, one was for a Frenchman who had settled long before in Buenos Aires, having become renowned and influential. His name was Paul Groussac. In 1885 Groussac had been named director of the National Library, which he converted into the most important in South America, on an equal footing with those in Europe. Many years later, when Jorge Luis Borges was appointed to that post, he declared that there was no need to buy a single book more, because as it had been conceived by his French predecessor it was the best library that could be created.

Thays and Groussac were examples of French immigration arrived in the River Plate with a high cultural level, and in some cases with a substantial economic standard. They were well received, and not before long, they prospered.

Differing from the British and the Germans, who assimilated slowly and with difficulty, or never at all, the French, like the Italians, became Argentine in the course of a few generations or even a few years. This did not mean that their love for their distant homeland had abated, as they showed it every time they could. Proof of this was given in the same year of Jacques' arrival, when the French community raised four hundred thousand francs to aid the victims of a flood in Paris. Clémençeau, a visitor at that time, asked himself why the French who had gone to North America in pursuit of fortune did not react in the same way; he supposed that the Latin trait fares better within a Latin environment.

Between 1850 and 1890 the French presence in the River Plate seemed more like colonization, or at least that is how it was reflected in the newspapers in France. Basques and Béarnese, who were a majority among French immigrants during those years, built the base for industry in Argentina. Although many of them chose to settle in Buenos Aires, vast numbers flocked to the provinces.

The Cuyo region, in the province of Mendoza, was one of their favorites. The town of San Rafael was known as a French colony, and in the neighboring province of San Juan the French became pioneers in the Argentine wine industry. Other immigrants settled in the northern provinces of Tucumán, Salta and Jujuy, where they started the sugar industry. Hileret is the best known name, as it remained a popular sugar brand.

Those who chose Buenos Aires as their destination invested in salting plants, in cereal mills and in other activities related to the agricultural business. The first packing houses were erected by immigrants from the Pyrenees, such as Terrason and Ollivier. The first printers and bookshop owners were French, as were the pioneers of the textile industry and of photography. Austere and tenacious, the French brought their traditional thrift, contributing their working methods and the characteristics of good living and courtesy which distinguish their culture.

Jacques began his visits with letters of introduction to the most prominent members of the French colony, given to him by his father.

Here he met with his first disappointments, because in some cases the welcome was ice-cold. Years later his friend Henri Becquerel would explain the reason; many good families in France got rid of their undesirable young members by sending them as far as they could, and that is where the River Plate was. These youngsters had earned a bad reputation, of abuse of hospitality and of absconding, with cash or with a daughter, and that accounted for the coldness that Jacques had experienced.

The only family that gave him a warm welcome was that of admiral García Mansilla (Eduarda's grandson), distant relatives of the Larminats through the La Fatisnerie branch. The García Mansillas led a high life and were very French; some time after, during a visit that Jacques paid them after his first trip to Neuquén, he recommended that they travel and contemplate those landscapes that he had marveled at, to which García Mansilla replied jovially: "We are delighted that there are Parisians willing to populate Patagonia, but let us go to Paris..."

With this family Jacques got to know the Palermo promenade where elegant society met to show off their luxurious automobiles and majestic carriages. To breathe fresh air, to enjoy nature, as a distraction and for conversation were mere excuses for the real purpose of this ceremony, which was to see and to be seen. Six rows of vehicles went to and fro along a distance of four hundred meters, almost touching each other both ways, while the rest of the avenues of the vast park remained deserted. Jacques would have wanted to go for a walk under those weeping willows of such delicate green, the *ombús*, eucalyptus and poplars, but etiquette imposed an established circuit, and to comply with ceremonial greetings. Almost all conversations were about marriages in the making. Jacques could not remember ever seeing so many beauties together, and dressed with such elegance.

Jacques' early friends were young foreigners like himself. One of them was Olivier de Malglaive, who had been in the country for some years and had become an expert in every trade, including the one of *langostero*, locust man, in other words inspector in the fight against the short-horned grasshopper. This young man would show up at friends' houses in Buenos Aires armed with a pair of enormous spurs, which he clanged *"pour épater le bourgeois"*, to surprise the public. He held long conversations with Jacques, and in his stories the strange and fascinating profile of the country would begin to take shape for his newly arrived friend.

Another young friend from those times was an Englishman, whom he evokes in a letter many years later. "Stanley Mallet goes from one whisky to another, comfortably seated alone in his fancy coach which he leaves behind once every five days, when he invites his coachman to eat and drink with him. The curious fact is that we met again much later, unknowingly, in the plains of Assas. He commanded a squadron of Hindi lancers; I was at the head of the 16th Dragoons. He would later become Lord Chancellor to the young princess Elizabeth, now queen of England, and later still he settled near Carlos Casares, in La Corona, a magnificent *estancia* which he managed very well. There he entertained the Prince of Wales, the future Duke of Windsor, and later also Reid, Trannack, and myself."

5

Apprenticeship in the Fields

Playing truco, *recollection of the Argentine countryside*

*J*ACQUES DID NOT STAY IN BUENOS AIRES for long. Anxious to escape the heat and dampness of the city, and to start his apprenticeship in the Argentine countryside, he accepted an invitation from another Frenchman, Jean Guichard. This compatriot offered him an *au pair* internship, that is to say, in exchange for food and lodging, at his *estancia Los Algarrobos*, north of Río Cuarto, in the province of Córdoba. Jacques set off at once, along abominable roads, taking a complete set of riding gear, which he had bought on the advice of another compatriot who had experience in traveling around Argentina. During this trip, which included long nights spent in the open, he was able to value the wisdom of the advice, because at night the riding gear became the gaucho's bed, the saddle pads serving as pillow.

Once he arrived at *Los Algarrobos,* Jacques found Guichard living in a precarious *rancho*[13], with his wife Marie Thérese, née Mademoiselle de Clermont, and a Belgian friend, Germaine Peltzer, from a

---

[13] Rancho: The typical dwelling of the Argentine gaucho. It is made of adobe, the unburnt sun-dried bricks, and roofed with straw and rushes. In its humblest version the floors are simply earth

family well known in the dairy business, and an English governess whom they called Daisy. Beside the house, in a tent, Jacques set up his quarters with two other apprentices, René Millet and Pierre Lemasson.

Guichard was a great bourgeois; his father and his father-in-law were millionaires, and gave him credit and then withdrew it with certain regularity. His fear, in the South American adventure he had set out on, was to give in to the lack of comfort and to lose the social refinement in which he had been born and lived. So he had established some rules of etiquette which everybody followed. For supper the head of the household wore a red dinner jacket with black trousers; his wife and Germaine, evening dresses; Lemasson ornamented himself with a monocle; only Millet, a plump young man with an impetuous personality, kept his working clothes on, "with a magnificently low neckline", as Jacques related with humor. On Sundays Millet disappeared to Río Cuarto, or to some other mysterious destination. He later married the pleasant Germaine Peltzer and returned to France.

The table where these dinners were held was a wooden box laid on the hard earth floor. The service was directed by a black maitre, impeccable, all dressed in white, including his gloves. His wife was the cook; she had a swarthy baby who one day fell into the cesspit and drowned.

According to the description made by Jacques in his letters to his family, the soil of the *estancia*, "slightly undulated, is covered by an American herb that grows in yellowish green clumps, the Puna grass, unwanted even by mules, all with a spattering of groves of carob and *chañar*[14] trees, the leaves of the latter having such keen edges that they can slice one's clothes, and are inhabited by green, blue and gray parrots". Jacques found old arrow points in that environment, which he collected.

---

[14] Chañar: A tree belonging to the leguminous family, noteworthy for its size and beauty.

Everything remained to be done at *Los Algarrobos*. Fences had to be built and alfalfa had to be sown without delay, because the hay to feed the draft mules had to be bought. And everything had to be made, if they did not want to live indefinitely in a tent. Work was exhausting, but exciting for someone as eager to learn as Jacques. Farmhands were patient with the three young Frenchmen, seared by the unforgiving sun of Córdoba in summer, especially good Millet's fat and rosy arms. Work days began before sunrise and ended at eight in the evening, with two hours' rest at midday. Jacques wrote to his family telling them that he had learnt to build wire fences, and also knew how to sow.

Guichard, fully assuming his role as pioneer, used to dress up with a pair of striped trousers made of Mexican leather and an enormous cowboy hat, together with a big white handkerchief around his neck. If he saw someone trespassing on his property he fired his revolver in the air; people in that area, used as they were to perfect calm, would be frightened by the shots. The apprentices were made to get up two hours before sunrise to fetch the mules from the packed cor-ral; the mules, all wild and identical, were never happy to see them. But the men had to wait for the sun to appear, so as not to run the risk of getting a well placed kick in the dark. When they became more dexterous the work was performed quickly, but Guichard, a man of principles, never accepted an alteration to the schedule, which made them lose a fair amount of sleep every morning.

Guichard was kind enough to give Jacques the most varied tasks, in which he sometimes joined; agriculture and the building of fences, which left his hands aching and bleeding, and also the assembling of agricultural machines, carpentry, the sowing of barley and saddling of mules. Jacques knew well that these animals were stubborn and distrustful, but were considered by country people as the most intel-ligent and the most efficient for the work. However, he was too much of a beginner to have them as his allies, and the animals seemed to mock his lack of experience. After some notorious failure a farmhand would say: "It seems the mules are laughing at you..."

Mules raise their upper lips in a gesture which seems filled with sarcasm. Anecdotes went around about the faithfulness, the intelligence and the commitment of mules. Jacques knew of a neighbor who sent his young son to plow early in the morning. The boy, very friendly with the six mules that pulled the plow, slept peacefully because they lined up and did the job alone. The problem was when midday arrived and the boy was still sleeping soundly; then the mules, perhaps overwhelmed by heat, or maybe just cunning, returned to their pens, dragging the fences and gates they encountered on their way. The farmhands said that when the boy got his spanking, the mules laughed heartily. Little by little Jacques began to understand these animals; the clue, he was told, was the exchange of breath between the mules and their master. Just as efficient was to treat them well, and to add patience. In the end the mules became companions and priceless helpers, capable of marching a hundred kilometers in one day carrying heavy packs.

During a short Holy Week holiday Jacques returned to Buenos Aires. As per custom, all cinemas and theaters showed versions of the Passion, all so vivid that he found them shocking, "with Chopin's funeral march for the scene of the Calvary, and Aida's for the Resurrection". So he returned to his favorite rounds in the Botanical Garden and the Zoo. As a contribution to the Centenary, the Hamburg Zoo had sent a Himalayan bear, a collection of birds and several serpents, one of these weighing one hundred kilos, six meters long and with a head as large as a dog's. But aside from these attractions, Jacques did not particularly enjoy the city. Everything for him was in the making, the beginnings were slow, and above all he was feeling the solitude and estrangement from his family. He indulged in observing, as he says in his letters, the people of Buenos Aires, so fond of theater, which offered performances by local companies, but also by many from abroad, including some performing in French and in Italian.

Upon returning to Guichard's *estancia*, constant and exhausting work took his mind off his impatience about his future. He found an unexpected tutor in a compatriot, Adolfo, a former seaman and excellent builder; Jacques learned from him, but what he later recalled most vividly was the language he spoke, which the man called 'castile', a mixture of French and Spanish which resulted in expressions ranging from the odd to the hilarious.

Jacques, who spoke almost no Spanish when he arrived in Buenos Aires, was becoming more familiar with his new language, and his own name, spoken by those who knew him, began to adopt the Spanish form, Santiago.

On March 25 he attended a cattle auction in the town of Río Cuarto, close to *Los Algarrobos*. The trip was made by gig, amid such clouds of dust as the young Frenchman had never seen before. The town was packed, and finding lodgings proved difficult.

Millet and Jacques slept on three planks laid on two trestles in a room which already accommodated twenty other men. The auction was lively, with about twenty thousand head of cattle. Watching riders lasso the animals and shove them was an absorbing show. There were also llamas, brought from Bolivia, which some parents bought for their children.

Everything contributed to Jacques' learning. But the adventure in the province of Córdoba did not last. His master lost access to credit, in spite of the references his father offered bankers.

Searching for new opportunities he accompanied Guichard to inspect land for rent in Passo, on the limit between the provinces of Buenos Aires and La Pampa. This trip, which otherwise bore no results, had an unfortunate outcome, because Jacques lost one of his most precious possessions, his camera. He would soon have another, and then others; throughout his life he kept his habit of recording the places he went to, in snapshots or in drawings.

Guichard proposed a partnership to start a dairy farm, which he would manage; taking in consideration how volatile his potential partner's fortune was, plus the man's lifestyle, Jacques concluded that the wisest move was to withdraw from the scene, and so they parted.

Back in Buenos Aires, and more conversant with his future job, he consulted some realtors about the price of land. He had no intention of purchasing any yet, because as he said in a letter "I am too much of a novice to dream of buying". He was informed that in the south of the provinces of Buenos Aires and Río Negro the drought was already in its third year.

In Patagonia there were good prospects for raising sheep, but far down, level with the Chilean town of Punta Arenas, winter meant three months of snow, nights were long and the wind never ceased. All possibilities lay open; the country possessed every climate and every landscape, but as it was difficult to arrive at a decision he postponed it.

He accepted a proposal from a new friend, also a Frenchman. This was Joseph de la Perrière, who had rented land close to Oncativo, between the town of Villa María and the city of Córdoba[15]. This was a small farm by the name of *La Mariquita*.

Along went Jacques, first crossing the province of Entre Ríos, where on the banks of the Paraná river many Frenchmen had settled and land was cheap. But the young adventurer was intimidated by the challenges of the region: to fight tick, foot and mouth disease, tuberculosis and locusts.

On April 25 Jacques arrived in Oncativo, where he rented a gig to get to *La Mariquita*. On the way he admired the woods of *chañar* and carob trees that grew endlessly westward, the amount of wild life and the yellowish tuff that surged in colorful bluffs. In some places immense saltpeter rocks white as snow emerged from the ground, while the Córdoba hills rose above the horizon, perfectly outlined in the stillness of the air.

Joseph de la Perrière was Guichard's exact opposite; he was polite, sensible, with neither pushing ambitions nor packing a revolver, and he managed his life with great calm. Careless with his

---

[15] Córdoba: Capital of the province by the same name

clothes, which grew yellow with time, he did not renew them until they fell in tatters. He wore a thick, black beard, which he never trimmed. Some years before he had traveled along the coast of Brazil, with a cousin of Jacques', Guillaume de Tristan. He had written the story of this journey in a pleasant little book which Jacques enjoyed reading, and which encouraged him further to pursue his objectives.

Joseph de la Perrière operated with very limited resources; he had but one laborer, a taciturn man, whom he had engaged shortly before, and whose past history included a murder. The Frenchman did his own cooking, but after frequent failure he decided to go to the city of Córdoba in search of a cook.

Jacques remained alone with the farmhand, who on one occasion caught an armadillo by its tail; this animal, slaughtered, disemboweled and cooked slowly inside its own covering with grease, turned out to be an excellent lunch. It reminded Jacques of the taste of pork; he also learnt that its wild flavor was abated by leaving it buried for a few days.

At last the boss returned with a cook, Felicia, an old *Cordobesa* who proved to be an absolute pearl, because not only was she familiar with all country traditions, but performed faultlessly. She cooked, washed, made different kinds of cheese and cold meats, manufactured candles that burnt to perfection, made soap with a foul smell, but also sheepskin cushions and a thousand other things. Her only vice was to drink black coffee by the gallon.

She seemed to know all that could be known about curative herbs, plus the traditional prescriptions. She cured migraine by sticking on the forehead little scraps of cigarette paper which she collected from the butts thrown by her boss. When de la Perrière tried to offer her unused paper, she rejected the suggestion with the contempt of a doctor faced with the advice of a novice.

The flora of the region offered a complete pharmacopoeia, which Jacques endeavored to learn. The fruit of the carob tree was used to treat indigestion, as it is a mild laxative. It is also efficient as an expectorant. The fruit of the *chañar* is excellent to stop bouts of coughing, and ideal to cure chronic catarrh, asthma and bronchitis. It can also be useful as a diuretic and to reduce inflammation of the urinary tract. Jacques was able to defeat a strong bronchitis with the aid of six daily cups of a potion made from boiled *chañar* leaves, sweetened with honey.

Arum is good against gout, sciatica, rheumatism and arthritis. Immersing one's feet in an arum bath mitigates sweat and bad odor, a practice never personally used by Felicia. An infusion of pennyroyal was used by the indians to speed up baby deliveries that were delayed, as an overall soothing agent and to treat heart palpitations and ear buzzing. *Suico* was an infallible remedy for diarrhea and stomach disorders. And an infusion of acacia never failed as an internal healer.

Forever eager to learn, Jacques took note of every one of Felicia's prescriptions. He used to bring to her every vegetable and animal he found, for her to pass judgment on its usefulness. He became very knowledgeable about the flora of the region, not so much with a curative objective, but to be able to ascertain the quality of the earth, its richness and humidity. The little grove close to the house became his favorite refuge, as it already was for many animals unknown to him: weasels, birds with yellow necks, magpies, and one day, a big gray toucan. Parakeets and parrots, a plague for plantations, were much more abundant.

There were such numbers of parrots that one day, having gone out hunting with de la Perrière, he downed twelve with a single shot from a 16 caliber shotgun, thus confirming his fame as a good shot. They went out nights hunting *vizcachas*[16], when they emerged from their immense subterranean warrens, which had innumerable entrances and sometimes extended for over a hectare. This big gray rodent, with its tail of stiff hairs, was very difficult to kill, even with

[16] Vizcachas: A large burrowing rodent related to the chinchilla

a shotgun; once wounded they would disappear into their caves, unassailable strongholds where at night there was tremendous activity. Jacques thought its meat, white, dry and fibrous, was mediocre, but it was eaten throughout the Pampas, prepared in a marinade of oil and spices.

Work consisted of revising the pasture patches, managing with the few tools available, keeping the fences upright, and every now and then, when a cow died, dragging the skinned carcass away with a cart. Once in the homestead, an "autopsy" was performed, which generally astonished the Frenchmen. If they asked their farmhands or their neighbors, these, with the gravity of university lecturers, would solemnly state that "it must have been a poisonous herb" or "the plague, for sure" and all deliberations ended when someone decided that the cow had died simply because it had to die.

One day, to test if he had learned his lessons, Jacques went into the corral and threw the lasso wide open over a group of horses that were

PHOTO: SANTIAGO DE LARMINAT (1952)

Lassoing

moving about him. He was ready for the jerk, but when it arrived it pulled him to the ground. After turning over four times and losing his glasses and some skin off his hands, he realized, amid the laborers' laughter, that he had lassoed four horses at the same time.

Among the memories from that time he recalled two neighbors, father and son, who visited them to buy some animals. "The son, a *nouveau riche*, deserved to be smacked. Influenced in extreme by a parody of social ascent, the youth looked with scorn at his father, who calmly took a piece of biscuit with his hand, while he did the same using a fork. In a few years the small family fortune would be squandered, and the grandson would again pick up the biscuit with his hands like his grandfather, in accordance with the proverb that circulated among immigrants in Argentina: "From one poor man to another poor man, two generations will suffice."

On the other hand Jacques liked the hospitality offered in the country, and the numerous formulas that expressed it. "This is your home", "now you know the way", common in a territory in which distances and the lack of lodgings made these offers indispensable. The village police officer visited them and upon departing said: "Oncativo is your home". Another neighbor whose surname was Nariz, which is Spanish for 'nose', used to touch his own when parting so his name would be remembered, saying: "Always at your service".

Among his observations, which he punctually communicated in his letters to his family, he mentioned the keen eye of the natives. They would see a point on the horizon and say "There's so and so coming". As a rule they recognized the horse, which was the first thing they recorded and which also lasted long in their minds. A conversation between two laborers would go thus: "Do you remember that man who came eight years ago during the branding season?" "The one who mounted a bay horse with three white legs?" "That's the one I mean".

The idea with which he had come to the country remained latent: to find a suitable place to start an agricultural and cattle breeding enterprise. But it was still necessary to learn more. And every opportunity was useful for this purpose. Jacques went to the city of Córdoba to see the director of the Agricultural School, a member of a well known French family by the name of Blacke-Belair, and obtained from him valuable information on the region. He made use of the visit for an excursion to the *sierras*, and was bewildered by the untouched beauty of La Cumbre. He traveled on a small railway line that ran through the hills. These appeared arid except for some places with luxuriant trees, a reminiscence of the Spanish *sierras*. He found the San Roque dam imposing, although due to a drought the level of the water was very low. After a night spent in Capilla del Monte he climbed the top of Mount Uritorco, which was the highest point in the region. He contemplated with admiration a landscape of low and leafy palm trees, which formed patches of green shade, over a layer of violets and other wild flowers.

Agricultural fairs were a good place to ask questions, to see and to learn. Jacques visited the one that was held at Villa María, and in September he traveled to Buenos Aires for the Annual Agricultural Show. He endeavored to leave nothing to chance, but knew that it would probably be chance that brought him the signal of his destiny. He evaluated carefully every place that was mentioned to him, and he did not hesitate to travel long distances to see for himself if the land was worth it. In a letter to his father he told him of his desire to know the south of the country, although "not too close to the Andes, where in fact the market is very small, but I would rather start bordering the Atlantic, where there is a greater population and looks better. I hope to go during the shearing season, because it is the best time to evaluate those lands".

He also considered the province of San Luis, the valleys in the province of La Rioja, and even further north. At the end of October he visited a compatriot, one of his best friends, George de Martrin Donos, who had offered him a position as an accounting employee in his *estancia La Totora* during shearing time. In that place Jacques once again experienced the harshness of the climate. After a winter of drought, a spring with rain in excess isolated Martrin Donos' *estancia*, hampering the transport of wool. Jacques drew a caricature of the moment when an enormous lorry, full of canvas bales with wool, overturned in the water and remained immersed in mire. In that *estancia* he met a sheep laborer, Gallardo Lavalle, who years later would be the first foreman of the Larminats' *estancia*, working for them until his death in 1926. This man was the son of an assistant captain of the Araucano indian chief Saihueque, who as a boy, it was said, had been captured by general Lavalle[17], who gave him his name and raised him in Buenos Aires. (It was also rumoured that in fact he was the general's son).

But the plains of the Pampas finally impressed Jacques as monotonous, and his desire to go further south was rekindled. He wanted to know "the famous Patagonia", where he would in the end find his destiny. The first impression was a good one. "Its deserts are picturesque. I was seduced by the simplicity and the poverty of its strange inhabitants. I would stay there all my life", he says in a letter.

Doctor Laure and his partners, the Kennard brothers, invited him to Chimpay, close to Río Negro, where only the valleys could be inhabited. It was enough to move ten kilometers away from a river for the landscape to undergo a complete change, it became an immense desert with thickets of *coirón*[18], the broom sedge, a few *chañares* and *piquillines*. This gray landscape that extended to the horizon had no paths; the few animals that inhabited it were wild and evasive: pumas, guanacos, ostriches, hares and herons.

Jacques recalled his experience with the words that Charles Darwin used when he explored this region: "the plains of Patagonia (...)

[17] Juan Lavalle (1797-1841) : An outstanding Argentine general who commanded troops in the liberation campaigns in Chile, Peru and Ecuador and served in the war against Brazil (1828). He eventually killed colonel Dorrego and lost his revolution against Rosas.
[18] Coiron: A thorny grass typical of Patagonia

are distinctive only for their negative characteristics: they have no dwellings, no water, no trees, no mountains; all they have is dwarf plants. Why then –and it has not only happened to me– have these arid deserts taken possession of my mind in such a way?".

The town of Chimpay, where the Río Negro meanders, was then little more than a railway station and a *pulpería* managed by two curious characters: Martin Bresler and Matuscka. The former became some time later a famous assassin, spending his life in different jails and escaping from them, building a reputation similar to that of Robin Hood, to end up insane; Matuscka was described by Jacques as a sparrow's brain on top of an elephant's body.

In Chimpay the young Frenchman witnessed a murder, and acted as qualified photographer for legal proceedings, but those were minor anecdotes. More important, in fact it was decisive, he met Martin's father, Daniel Bresler, an ex-Boer commander who invited him to join an expedition he was preparing to go further south in Patagonia. Jacques accepted, and they left shortly after, from the city of Neuquén, a caravan of six horsemen and two more in a cart. Commander Bresler was going to take possession of the land he had obtained from the State on the banks of Lake Lácar; two thousand five hundred hectares of fiscal land, apart from an area for summer grazing, with excellent pastures surrounded by woods. Later he would found the *Quechuquina estancia* in that land.

During the journey Jacques had to face his first difficulties with the widely advertised Patagonian wind. Lighting a fire to cook or to take *maté* was almost impossible, because the implacable wind would put out the fire, and if it did not blow it out, strenuous efforts were necessary to prevent the sparks from starting a forest fire. The wind would blow away their clothes, and cold, sand and dust that seeped in from everywhere prevented their sleep. Every task became doubly difficult. The mildest horses became restless and even saddling or tying them to the carts was troublesome. Sand hovering in the air darkened the sun, and the thicker grains hit mercilessly against the dusty masks in which their faces had transformed. Only sheep, in accordance with their habit, grazed facing the wind, as their height allowed them to shelter behind the broom sedges. Wild animals sought refuge in the narrow paths among the rocks or inside their dens, which prevented hunting them. When the wind blew without stop for several days it shattered the nerves of the most even tempered men.

In spite of such an unpropitious introduction, Jacques was reaching his goal.

Early Steps in Patagonia

Etienne de Larminat on the banks of lake Lácar, 1911

*T*HE FIRST IMPRESSION JACQUES DREW CONCERNING the region of San Martín de los Andes, and above all of lakes Lácar and Lolog, which he communicated to his family, was that humid land was scarce, and so full of trees that the space available for agriculture and raising cattle was minimal; however, pastures were abundant. Towards the east there was a region of plains more or less rocky and very windy, with patches of isolated thick clumps of *coirón*, very bad for animals. This land was inferior to the one at the back of the more humid valleys, where wheat and alfalfa would grow well.

Some of the best land he saw in his exploration belonged to the Chilean-Argentine Commercial and Cattle Breeding Corporation, whose director, Mr. Schloesinger, lived in Valparaiso, Chile. This was the person Jacques began to deal with, when he decided at last that the time had arrived to settle on land of his own. This *estancia*, called *Cerro de los Pinos*, Pine Trees Mount, had a spread of four thousand hectares of excellent soil, especially for sheep, with relatively wide spaces to sow cereals and alfalfa. It was on the Chimehuin river, a sub-tributary of the Limay, some eight or nine leagues from San

Martín de los Andes, and close to what would almost inevitably be the course of a future railway.

San Martín de los Andes and Junín de los Andes, the two closest towns, had been set up as border forts when general Roca concluded his final expedition against the native indians, and the purpose had been to put a limit to Chilean claims for territory. At that time, little over a decade since their foundation, they were each a hamlet with a few dwellings and some small vegetable farms surrounding the town square, each with a police station and a *pulpería*[19]. San Martín de los Andes had recently been turned over to civil government and the first school, post office and Justice of the Peace were being established.

"Cerro de los Pinos". The name has its origin in a peak with cypress trees in the middle of the fields, close to an area of big forests. The terrain is markedly uneven, interspersed with *mallines*[20] and slopes with grass which looks tough and unattractive at first sight, but which is very nutritive for cattle. At the moment of purchase there were some apple trees, many natural fountainheads, and some buildings.

In a letter to his father Jacques mentioned his idea of engaging a French couple; the woman would take care of the house, and the man should be a good asset as a worker. He also thought that he would need three French laborers, with whom he intended to train the local staff who at the moment "work in a highly inefficient way", although he admitted the need to engage some at least, for specific tasks to be performed on horseback. In a paragraph aside, he said that he missed both La Hardonière and his family. "There are times when I wonder if Algiers would not have been better...". But he added that these doubts assailed him only when the wind had altered his nerves.

His father answered celebrating his son's energy, congratulating him on his travels and work, but on the subject of purchasing that land, he did not hide his misgivings. Such an isolated place seemed to

---

[19] Pulpería: Pub, general store.
[20] Mallines: patches of humid lowland with very tender weeds.

him an excessive risk; if the railway took too long to arrive, a circumstance which seemed very probable given the difficult stretches of rock that it would have to overcome, his son would spend many trying years before being able to set up a family.

And this was not his sole concern. "Which is the real future of that country? Will it be able to develop fully? What are its resources? Those animals fattened on grass, won't they arrive skin and bones at consumer centers? As regards Chile, the map seems to indicate that the Andes are a great barrier. Is that so? Are there by any chance centers where the grain and cattle may be sold?"

Jacques' father recommended that his son study carefully the subject of transport in both directions. He also put forward innumerable questions regarding the altitude of San Martín de los Andes and the closeness of townships and cities. He suggested his son should put in doubt his sense of esthetics: "plain fields are ugly, but very good; nobody wants mountains for agriculture".

And he cautioned him against premature owner's grandeur recalling La Fontaine's fable about the frog who wanted to be as big as an ox. He ended modestly: "Please receive, my son, these reflections of mine as an aid to yours, which are the ones that matter, because concerning the site you will have at your disposal elements to judge which are alien to me. Your brothers and sisters agree with you and they feel tempted by a region less monotonous than the Pampas plains. Selecting land that is waiting for the railway may be the most judicious choice, ready for the installation of our family outside of France." And, if finally Jacques' decision was to buy in the region of San Martín de los Andes, he asked him for "all possible details: general topography, extension, population, big game hunting".

In fact, Jacques' perspective proved right. Patagonia, between the end of the military campaigns and the early decades of the twentieth-century, had been an isolated territory, lacking communication. When oil exploitation began, around 1912, finding a solution to this problem became an urgent matter. The boom of the automobile encouraged the

FOTO: SANTIAGO DE LARMINAT (1911)

Lake Lácar

construction of roads fit for traffic, as the existing ones were only suitable as cattle paths. The first railway of the region was the one which united Bahía Blanca, south of the province of Buenos Aires, with the town of Zapala, close to the first slopes of the Andes. The British who owned Great Southern Railway obtained the concession of this branch line in 1896 with an important stretch of land on both sides of the tracks, apart from freedom to determine the course, tax free importation during fifty years, the right to construct and exploit other branches and the right to use nearby rivers. The track ends in Zapala were laid on July 2, 1913, and the first train arrived in the following year, transforming the region into a center of trade and development of economic activities.

Jacques had already made up his mind, but he could not telegraph the news to his family because land speculation was already afoot, and to buy the land he had selected, the best one available, he had to keep his decision hushed. On February 2, 1910, he signed the provisional deed for the purchase of Cerro de los Pinos, making the first deposit of two thousand pesos.

In the next letter to his father he announced that the purchase had already taken place, and that he had also bought some sheep. This last operation had been carried out through Daniel Bresler, whom he called "my Boer commander". "I have absolute trust in him; he will buy four thousand sheep at three pesos, a unique opportunity since they are the product of the liquidation of the company". He was referring to the Chilean-Argentine Corporation that had sold the land to him.

But Santiago knew little about the personality of frontier people, and had not fully measured the rapacious cunning of the Boer, who had no qualms about swindling him. Bresler bought the sheep at two pesos and fifty cents, but invoiced them at three to Jacques –who was busy with papers in Valparaiso and Buenos Aires– and kept the difference. He rented some land to fatten them and put a shepherd, Gregorio Pinel, to take care of them.

Jacques in turn did not waste his time in Buenos Aires, which was getting ready for the Centenary celebrations. All his efforts were aimed at buying fiscal land to add to that he had already purchased. He wrote to his father: "I think we are excellently positioned to obtain from the government land in the Andes, which they sell at five pesos (six, with the commission) payable in five years, and it is a matchless deal. Unfortunately obtaining it is very difficult. But I have high hopes. Bresler endorses me before the government; they consider us among the few serious settlers in the Andes. We cannot get more than a league per person, but perhaps with Etienne's name we will be able to buy more. I have in my plans two fields for summer pastures and others for agriculture. They would both complement to perfection our Cerro de los Pinos, as they are close by and only two leagues away from San Martín de los Andes."

On March 29, 1910, two weeks after his twenty-first birthday,

Jacques entered his application at the Ministry of Agriculture in Buenos Aires. After this he allowed himself a few days' rest going about the city, which he found surprisingly changed.

In the year of the Centenary a construction craze overtook Buenos Aires. Great French-like and Italian-like mansions were built; monuments were inaugurated, new streets were opened and avenues broadened; the excavations for the first subway were under way, and new parks were designed. The atmosphere was one of euphoria. The passing of Halley's comet was awaited eagerly; if in other countries this event inspired fear and was a cause for suicide, in Argentina it was considered a signal from the heavens announcing a promising future. The comet passed over Buenos Aires at dawn on May 19, and the whole population waited sleepless. The celestial body blessed May Week, the much awaited event when the country would show its achievements and its greatness.

The protest action staged by anarchists failed to cloud the celebrations. The plan for a revolutionary strike was relegated to the inside sections of the newspapers, while front pages were devoted to the visits of prominent personalities, the most conspicuous being the *infanta* Isabel de Borbón, sister to Alfonso XII and aunt of the then king Alfonso XIII, whose visit sealed reconciliation with Spain.

The *infanta* arrived a few days before the celebrations and lodged in the De Bary palace, on the Alvear Avenue. Accompanied by large retinues, presidents and ministers from neighboring countries were arriving. The activity was feverish; here and there cornerstones for future monuments were being laid: the Spaniards', the Italians', Christopher Columbus'...

Celebrations were not limited to prominent people. Popular feasts were being prepared, with distribution of food and clothes, free theater shows, fireworks, cinema. Special horse races were organized at the Palermo Racecourse, among them the Great Centenary Prize.

When the big day arrived, May 25, twenty thousand Argentine and foreign troops paraded in Plaza de Mayo, cheered by a large crowd. In the evening the opera Rigoletto was sung at the Colón opera house, and journalists agreed that never before had the theater looked so impressive.

Jacques described the celebrations in his correspondence to his family. In his answer, his father encouraged him, apprehensive that the inconveniences and solitude might breed disappointment. "I think that when your two brothers get there, and you can exchange views with them, life for you will become very different". The Larminat family spirit is present in that sentence.

Jacques was an innovator; he did not like to tread on known paths, and had launched himself into this adventure with great zeal. But he was very young, little more than a teenager, and having to manage a question of such responsibility all by himself must have been very difficult. Although he was genial and sociable, he was also very distrustful, as were all Larminats. He anxiously awaited the arrival of his brothers, with the certainty that once they were together the wheels which would turn them into pioneers would start to roll.

There can be no doubt that Jacques was the driving force in this story, and there is no sense in speculating what would have happened if he had had to face the challenge by himself. It is very possible that he would have attained his objectives all the same, because he had the mettle of those people who make their dreams come true. But as things unraveled, the fruits were the result of the brothers' union and affection.

The letter from his father mentioned above continues as follows: "Deep in your soul you will have a legitimate satisfaction when you see the prosperity of your family in the present times and in the future thanks to these early years of efforts. My Cocot, there shall be something to compensate generously for the miseries, and pay for the tough moments that you shall inevitably go through". And he ends up talking about La Hardonière, where trees were in bloom, the golden genista blazed in every corner and a fine scent of pine trees wafted in the air.

Jacques' father did not limit himself to giving advice and encouragement. He had already engaged a couple, the Ligers, and had thrilled them with the prospect of traveling to Argentina.

Etienne sat for his last exam and graduated as an engineer in the renowned École des Mines, so he was ready to start on his journey and join his brother. The sisters, from Jean de Larminat's second marriage, were being introduced in society. Legislative elections in France left the Chamber with a majority of radicals, but, according to *Le Figaro*, the radicals had become sensible and had more moderate ideas, a fact which is common in parties that arrive in power. The republicans and the progressive parties raised the flag of social claims. Jean wrote to Jacques: "Elections have been decidedly better than what the Ministry of the Interior expected, and a majority of deputies have declared their support for proportional representation for the minority, freedom of teaching, against income tax and against the State's manipulation. How can people vote for them? That is what we are, obviously."

7

From Buenos Aires
to Cerro de los Pinos

Plaza de Mayo, Buenos Aires, 1910

ON JULY 23, 1910 BROTHERS ETIENNE AND André arrived in Buenos Aires to join Jacques on his Patagonian adventure. The three lodged at the Frascati Hotel, whose rates had been raised to take advantage of the great demand the Centenary celebrations brought. Although the newcomers wanted to travel as soon as possible to Cerro de los Pinos, they were delayed in Buenos Aires by the paper work involved in signing the land title deed. They also needed time to apply for the two leagues of fiscal land Jacques was after, the Grande and the Lolog estates. The application lay dormant in the Ministry, and the Larminats would still accumulate several kilos of stamped paper before they abandoned the prospect.

Jacques, Etienne and André took advantage of the delay to tour the city: the Zoo and the Botanical Garden, the port, the Palermo neighborhood and the Universal Exhibition. At this fair they were most impressed by the colossal agricultural machinery manufactured in the United States. There were harvesters equipped with automatic grain removers, with an enormous tube where an air spout blew out all the dislodged chaff and sent it a good distance away; mechanical shearing machines with large tentacles which ended in a double row of teeth; steam locomotives with oversize wheels that dragged a dozen loaded wagons. To fight against locusts, a "locusticide" contraption had been manufactured in Argentina, with huge blades that beat the ground with formidable blows. The Larminat brothers bought more modest utensils: a small forge with an anvil, a hand mill which yielded very white flour, and little more.

The only way to go by train to their destination (with the exception of the last lap) was to travel to Santiago de Chile, carry on southwards to Valdivia city and cross the mountain range to San Martín de los Andes. Departure was delayed because of the weather; they were at the mercy of the snow that blocked the *Transandino* line, and had no choice but to wait. At the hotel they met *estancieros* who had come to the Exhibition from remote places in the country. They came across Juan de Dios Reille, who in the company of Malglaive was waiting, as they were, to start for Río Colorado, where he proposed to study the possibilities of irrigating the area. Etienne on his part met with co-students from the Mines School. The encounters were so many, so numerous, and so merry the company, that they did not regret having to spend some weeks before setting out.

Not all was fun. Etienne registered his signature at the River Plate French Bank, opening the first family account in the country. They visited the Ministry of Agriculture and had a first inkling, given the tortuous slowness of the applications, that they would have to return countless times. They applied for the approval of the mensuration of the estate, and bought the items they judged necessary for a long trip and an extended stay away from civilization. The two newcomers discovered that they had not brought a sufficient pairs of the big, sturdy, Saint Hubert hunting shoes, and had to have those bought locally reinforced, because "the shoes that we have found here will not last long". Likewise local underwear impressed them unfavorably: "stockings can only be used once".

As a consequence, they began to include in their correspondence long lists of requests, because they thought that almost always it should be more convenient to get the goods sent from France, for quality and for price, even taking into account the Customs surcharge. So they asked for tools and arms; a La Française carbine, for the Andes, for which they could get cartridges in Buenos Aires. It was also advisable to carry a shotgun to hunt ducks, wild geese and ostriches. Also a Colt 45, because bullets were easy to get, and although that weapon was branded as heavy and uncomfortable, it was not difficult to get used to its company, and it was a lot less dangerous to load than the small pocket toys that most people used. In fact, they were used to the French Army revolver, but they doubted the possibility of getting bullets for it. They also asked for an English saddle, good squared paper, notebooks and copybooks, Faber pencils and erasers.

Walking about Buenos Aires they came across stores where they purchased traveling bags and double knapsacks, cartridge pouches "with the pocket on the left", big knives that could be used to behead and butcher animals, and also for eating purposes. Jacques had ordered in the province of Mendoza muzzles, halters, head gear, reins, hobbling straps and lassos. Hides had to be bought in the country, where they were of a better quality and more resistant because they were hand worked, stretched and softened during a long time. Nor could pharmacy purchases be forgotten, though they were selected at random, since they had to wait until practice and experience showed them what was necessary. They bought serum against tetanus and also against snake bites, syringes, aspirins, quinine, paregoric elixir and potassium permanganate to make hydrogen peroxide. And also ponchos and neck scarves. However, they were unable to get, in spite of a thorough search, herd drivers' glasses, necessary when riding through clouds of dust or against the wind.

On July 30 they signed the final deed for the purchase of Cerro de los Pinos. Once the luggage was ready it was sent via the Villalonga agency to Neuquén, from where it would be carried to the Andes. Nevertheless, due to the rigor of that winter, they would be unable to engage a cart driver before October, so that the three youngsters would have to make do with the means contained in their travel bags.

But the train did not seem ready to depart. Newspapers published alarming news about the *Transandino* railway; trains blocked by snow, passengers without food or heating with a temperature several degrees below freezing point, plus indignant claims against the Company and the State. It seemed that there would be no trains until the situation improved.

Some favorable change seemed to take place by August 7, because the Company decided to run the risk and send another train. The arrival of the Larminat brothers at the station was anomalous, because although they carried little luggage, before they got there a porter climbed onto the coach as it was moving, anxious to get business before his competitors, and the coachman, to make him get off, insulted him and threatened him with a knife. This led to him losing control of the vehicle, which ran over a street sweeper. A policeman appeared on the scene, arrested the coachman and asked the passengers for their address, to call them as witnesses. With great presence of mind Jacques gave him an imaginary address: Valparaiso street, any number. They took another coach, arrived at the station, jumped on the train that was leaving for Mendoza and sighed deeply, greatly relieved. They were on their way.

A few hours later, seated in the dining car, they were watching the plains extend in all directions until they disappeared on the horizon. In some parts the landscape was colored with the yellowish green of mown alfalfa; then everything darkened, when they crossed fields that had been plowed. The homesteads of *estancias* were spotted in the distance, half hidden in the midst of wooded surroundings. At regular intervals the train stopped at a station, which was identical to all the previous ones. Further on grass substituted alfalfa, and hares and ostriches came into view. Soon they were crossing marshes and salt flats. In the evening, when they had reached the province of San Juan, lying in uncomfortable berths, they felt suffocated; the air was becoming dense. On the following morning they found everything covered by a fine dust, and the landscape had changed. Now there were dales with dried underbrush spattered here and there. Towards the west the Andes began to show their profile, a black wall ahead, a white wall behind.

In Mendoza they changed trains and carried on in the *Transandino*, which they regarded as "infamous". They had almost no space for their scant luggage, and even less for themselves. At breakfast part of the passengers had no choice but to squeeze against each other in a corner, to leave room for the others to eat. Conversation could be heard in English, German, French and Spanish.

Following the course of the Mendoza river, which meandered frothily along the bottom of the valley, the train began to climb the mountain. Suddenly the slope became more pronounced, the sound of a loud stutter heralded a choking locomotive, and progress slowed. The sky darkened and cold set in. The peaks around were craggier, the train kept slowing, often coming to a halt. It was snowing. They finally got to Puente del Inca, where the train came to a stop. Five minutes went by, then ten, then half an hour. A passenger went up front to find out what was happening; he returned very excited and announced: "The tracks are blocked. The train cannot carry on." There was general consternation, but the news was confirmed.

Luckily they were at Puente del Inca, a station with thermal waters that had guests in summer, and close to the station there was a large hotel (destroyed by a storm years later) where passengers arrived panting, due to the limited oxygen at that altitude, and in a whirlwind of snow. They found accommodation at the hotel, where the Larminats were given a spacious room which they judged comfortable. Later, at supper, some of the passengers began to protest loudly, demanding positive answers to their queries.

Everybody ended up taking part in the discussions, in which indignant exclamations mingled with appeals for calm. There were contradictory proposals voiced: to return to Mendoza in the locomotive, to cross to Chile with a pack of mules. Someone announced that he would write a letter to the Minister, another suggested sending an article to a newspaper. The Larminats were displeased by the fact that the most loud-mouthed were the French.

That night, a group of passengers, convinced that the only way not to wake up frozen was to plug every opening in their room and light a brazier, survived by a miracle.

Next day the deliberations continued, and a majority, having reached the conclusion that the situation was untenable, pressed the station master until he agreed to send a train back to Mendoza. Off went the troublemakers, while the Larminats, with a few others, calmly stayed in Puente del Inca. Meanwhile one of the passengers, without a word to anyone, found a guide and two mules and crossed over to Chile.

The weather began to get better, and during the days that followed the three young Frenchmen spent their time on excursions around the vicinity and took photographs. The region impressed them as curious, especially given the lack of vegetation, represented solely by some thick plants that prospered flat against the ground.

Most of the people who had remained at the hotel were French. Two engineers who were on their way to La Paz, Bolivia, another who was going to explore some gold mines in the north of Neuquén, an Englishman whose sense of humor soon made him unbearable, a Spaniard, and a few Argentines. They killed time playing bridge.

A locomotive arrived with a plough to open a path in the snow. But the machine plough was out of order, and its only use was to carry the men who did the work with shovels.

The Larminats, with the inspector's permission, went with these men up to the township of Las Cuevas. It was a most exciting journey, on an open platform upon wheels at the mercy of nature, during which they passed by several teams of tough-faced diggers, dressed with heavy clothes and shod with scraps of hairy hide tied with lengths of leather straps.

Etienne and the Transandino blocked by snow

Puente del Inca: waiting for a solution

When they returned they were told that the arrival of a train coming from Chile had been announced by telephone. They somehow imagined that there would be no problem for that train's engine to make a switch and take them to their destination. Having had enough of the experience in low-oxygen air at high altitude, they felt cheered by this prospect. Furthermore, the bill at the hotel was already quite steep. The price was an abuse, no doubt, but they found consolation in the thought that in Mendoza they would have had to pay the same, without enjoying the magnificent scenery of that environment.

They carried their luggage to the station, certain that they would succeed in getting to Santiago de Chile. The train arrived, but neither persuasion nor threats had any effect upon the conductors.

The chief, an Englishman, had no intention of diverting from his established course, and carried on to Mendoza. The grounded passengers remained with their melancholy, looking westward, where menacing clouds loomed again, and cursed the hotel, the climate and British inflexibility.

But it did not take long for another train to appear, and this one was coming in the right direction. All the known faces that had returned to Mendoza were aboard. At first, the joy of being able to resume their journey made them forget the attitudes that had annoyed them; the three young Frenchmen boarded the train in exhilaration, and it was then that they recalled the defects that had made them detest their travel companions, as they discovered that there was no room either for them or their luggage. But they would not get off again. Somehow they found room, and the train started on its way.

At Las Cuevas they were stopped by a party of Customs officials who, by their looks, suggested the bands of renegades who according to hearsay were the scourge of the region. These men took their time with an Englishman whose papers were not in order. Somebody shouted, exasperated: "Get him off the train and let's carry on!". The head of the party turned around towards the impatient character and said, with disquieting coldness: "One more word, and it will be you whom I shall get off... and the rest of the passage."

At last they went through the tunnel across the boundary, and arrived, late in the evening, at the hotel Los Andes, hungry and tired. There they spent the night and on the next morning boarded another train to Santiago de Chile. In the daylight they noticed the difference in the landscape; from the flatness of the Argentine countryside and the barrenness of its mountain range to a labyrinth of green slopes, valleys at the bottom of which flowed streams skirted by willow trees and mimosa.

Except for a touch of local color such as the great candelabra-like cactus, and the backdrop of snow-capped mountains behind them, the landscape evoked in them the etchings of the Alps. But they were in a South American country, a fact which was confirmed by the sorry state of the tracks, which led to the train having to be dragged by three engines.

They arrived in Santiago de Chile at midday. They had been recommended the Oddo hotel, but it was packed. They got rooms at the Hotel de France, which in spite of its name they found lowly, and the food downright bad. The rooms, like in almost all hotels at that time, were dark but spacious.

However, they went out for a walk in the city and were delighted by the fineness of light and the spring-like temperature, with the added exotic effect produced by the unavoidable black mantillas in which all women wrapped themselves, from twelve year-old girls to women in their eighties. From behind they all looked the same, like nuns, and the Frenchmen could never guess if when they turned around they would meet the vivacious eyes of a young girl or the dry and consumed features of an ancient woman. Feminine headgear was also identical: a black scarf tied under the chin, enhancing the chubby curve of the cheeks. The city was constructed with the same checkerboard design as Buenos Aires, but at the end of every street the slope of a mountain would appear before the eyes. They liked the city, and would have stayed on for a few days, especially to attend a series of concerts by the famous violinist Jan Kubelik, with whom they had shared the refuge at Puente del Inca. But the urgency to get to Cerro de los Pinos prevailed and they got onto the train once more.

As they progressed southwards stations with increasingly rare names followed one after the other: Tinguiririca, Perquilauquen, Niquen, Pillaulelbun, Pitrufquen. They observed that the countryside bristled with corpses of charred trees, sometimes reduced to a black stake, sometimes still shaking two or three wrung limbs. The reason was that fires were started to produce fields fit for sowing, and that scene, mournful for the tree-loving Frenchmen, was the price to be paid for progress.

The landscape changed when the first *colihue*[21] canes appeared, which to them resembled bamboo, with the difference that these were full canes. The fields that had been set on fire for clearance began to alternate with woods that remained untouched, finally linking to form on both sides of the tracks the continuous foliage of a virgin forest.

Valdivia, the city where they got off the train, seemed to them quite peculiar. The streets were deep mire, and for the vehicles to move, planks had been laid on the surface, more or less in a straight line. The vehicles which dared advance over these precarious foot-bridges had to resort to all kinds of capers, which offered observers tremendous fun. It was worse where there were no planks. They saw carts sunk to the axles unloading sacks of flour while the oxen, with their legs invisible in the mud, ruminated calmly.

But mud was not the worst part. Almost half the city had recently been destroyed by fire. Skeletons of agricultural machines and remains of houses were everywhere. What was left of a store that sold umbrellas seemed a cave occupied by monstrous spiders.

They stopped at the Schuster Hotel, which they described as infectious. German food, which both fills and is treacherous made them desist. As a consequence, they wanted to leave Valdivia as soon as possible. Their first action was to visit the San Martín company, to find out what facilities they could get to continue their journey. The person in charge, a certain Carmino, did not seem very encouraging. With a doleful voice he declared: "There are no horses. They have all died, because there is no grass." When asked how such a thing could happen, he answered: "This is not the province. In the provinces there is grass, here there is none. That is why all of our horses are dead." The clue to the riddle was in the difference the natives made between "provinces" and "Andes". When the Frenchmen asked why such thick fence wire was used in that area, the answer was: "Because here we are not in the provinces. It is very cold at these altitudes, and thicker wires are necessary."

[21] Colihue: Local bamboo, *Chusca culeou.*

As the train was not to leave for a few days, they made an expedition to Corral, a small port at the entrance of the bay at the end of which Valdivia stood. They visited blast furnaces which impressed them with their size and activity. The San Martín company exploited them to the limit, but as the source of energy was exclusively firewood, the brothers perceived sadly that it would not be long before all woods in the region disappeared.

Another attraction in Corral was whale catching. It was end of season, but they were able to see the great stores of oil that had been collected, and the beaches were covered with enormous skeletons.

The three brothers went for long walks in the neighboring woods, which they found considerably depleted. It struck them that almost all trees were perennials, but with leaves of a green color and a freshness that would have seemed incompatible with that type of vegeta-

PHOTO: SANTIAGO DE LARMINAT (1910)

Whalers in Valdivia

116

tion. All the leaves had a penetrating scent which reminded them of coriander, of turpentine, and other smells.

At last they departed. The San Martín company train consisted of an engine followed by a kind of big freight wagon onto which horses, luggage and passengers were loaded. They did not travel a long stretch because the line ended a few leagues from lake Riñihue. There they got off and remained in the company of a one-eyed station master, who lived with his wife in a hut made with logs and iron sheets. Rain forced them to seek shelter in this elementary dwelling, where the good lady made fried cakes, a local biscuit which to them was a discovery.

But the horses that they had asked for to continue their progress did not arrive, and the rain was growing stronger. When they had almost decided to carry on by foot, one, two... three... horses appeared, and a mule, followed by a bearded and jovial little man. They saddled the horses and loaded the mule, an operation which took its time. They donned their ponchos and mounted. But André's horse obstinately refused to move, in spite of all the spurring and whip lashing. Far from moving forward, the animal suddenly went back, in a spiral, dangerously approaching the great pit that ran beside the railroad tracks. The scene was repeated three times, which the one-eyed station master found very funny. Until the farmhand resolutely clubbed the animal on the head, an action which instantly made the horse mild as a sheep.

The march began through the woods, under a heavy rain. They did not take long to realize that the most convenient course was to let the animals decide for themselves, which was better than following their riders' orders. They went over fallen timber, they got mud up to their bellies in stretches of soft mire, they ascended rocky bluffs full of obstacles, to then slide almost seated along slopes of clay, while the wet branches beat the riders' faces like whips and the ponchos became increasingly heavier.

They could have never been able to tell the road they were taking. They meandered between trees, climbed ceaselessly in rounds until

117

they saw in the distance, through fog, a lake; then, a quick descent, followed by wading across a pebble-ridden stream that required audacious acrobatics.

At last they arrived at a house on the shore, with a wooden pier at the back and a small vessel that floated at a certain distance: that was Riñihue. They were welcomed with courtesy by the ship's captain, Bouder, a big bearded man who looked like a Breton seaman, and who lived in the company of numerous pigs and a surly Araucano woman.

Bouder informed them that a certain Ovalle, who lived in Huechulaufquen and was the supplier of horses, had gone to Collilelfú summoned by the Justice of the Peace, because his servant had poisoned himself with strychnine. The post was partly deserted because of this affair.

They crossed the Riñihue lake in the captain's ship. As the rain continued, they saw nothing more than the woods that skirted the lake, interminable walls of trees which were becoming increasingly sparse. In Huechulaufquen they found a big wooden house, more like a shed. Inside, in the middle of the earth floor, in a square pit, a small fire was burning. Behind the fire, Ovalle's old wife, and in a corner, the corpse of the poisoned man. As the Frenchmen had already experienced in those posts, there were no horses, and nothing to eat.

Before saying goodbye Bouder told them that three leagues from there, on the margin of the Panguipulli, in a place called Chan Chan, lived a man called Zapata who could have horses. The three Larminat brothers decided to set off without delay. But to get to Chan Chan they had to cross the Enco river. They walked carrying on their shoulders luggage and saddles, and crossed the Enco in a raft tied with chains to a cable that traveled the river diagonally. The strong current made the crossing dangerous, but they arrived safely on the opposite shore. They left their belongings against a tree, covered with an iron sheet, and carried on.

They walked across the wood, always under a rain that at that stage had turned their ponchos into leaden mantles, slipping and sinking in the spongy slime. Every now and then they heard a creak-ing, which announced a tree crashing to the ground, sometimes dragging two or three others with it. The frequency of this scene explained the reason why telephone lines did not work in winter.

Three hours later a donkey appeared on their track and began to trot ahead of them; then a pig, until finally they discovered a small wooden house with a chimney with a faint column of smoke. That was Chan Chan. Behind, an arm of the Panguipulli lake could be seen, surrounded by great forests blurred by rain.

But in Chan Chan they found nothing more than an old and sick woman; her husband had gone to Collilelfú. What could be done? They could see no other solution but to continue on foot to Molco. Before going on their way, they asked the woman for something to eat. The answer was that there was nothing in the house. But half an hour later they were served a chicken soup that did them a world of good.

When they were about to depart Zapata arrived. He said he had two pack mules, and offered to carry their belongings the next day to Molco. So the Frenchmen decided to spend the night with these good people, who in spite of their few resources made their stay as comfortable as was possible, making beds for them, real beds, in one of the corners of the big house.

On the following morning the rain had stopped. There was a bright sun, and the three brothers, set off with renewed optimism on the second stage of their travels across the beautiful Chilean forests.

The road bordered lake Panguipulli on a cornice, along a branch which took them to Molco. Upon arrival in this place they were unable to find a single soul. They had almost lost hope when the company employee who lived there, a man called Oscar Cruzat, appeared in a boat. He offered them a room to spend the night, but there were no horses. He told them the animals were so skinny that nobody could dream of using them. Meanwhile Zapata had brought their luggage and the saddles with his two mules, and had bidden farewell.

Again they were on foot, and again it was raining. They decided to wait for the weather to change before carrying on. They could stay in Molco, where they had food and lodging. They went for a ride on a canoe across the lake, and then through exuberant forests where each trunk served as support for a vegetation of big leafy moss, of ferns and honeysuckle vines with red flowers. Cruzat taught them to distinguish the main arboreal species of the region. The most remarkable was the *coihue*[22], whose end was a smooth trunk extended along a single stretch, with branches like sunshades with very fine foliage, and the myrtle, which prospered on the edge of the lake and spread out tortuous, twisted, orange colored limbs, growing under water like tentacles. The Larminats took a great number of photographs.

These excursions proved useful, because at the home of a neighbor, don Guillermo Ramual, they found two horses with which they could take their luggage up to Fuy, some twenty-three kilometers away. So off they went, armed with three loaves of bread and canned tuna fish.

The road progressed along beautiful *coihues*, which framed the snow-capped silhouette of the Mocho volcano. They crossed a small rush by a ford, and further on, upon arriving at the river Fuy, they had to use a bridge of uncertain safety; between two wooden supports that still conveyed some sense of firmness a series of planks had been laid, forming a steep curve downwards, where the river flowed, white with foam. With each step the bridge creaked, swung, and seemed about to collapse. But the people who lived in the vicinity had assured them that the two steel cables from which the bridge hung could withstand any test, and they got to the other side.

They stopped by a brook, to eat the bread and tuna fish. A little further on they left the great forests and the enclosing bamboo foliage, to cross the Huylahuinta plain, from where they admired an impressive waterfall of the river Fuy. From that point on the road worsened, and it started to snow. They progressed painfully; descending along an immaculate snow-covered slope only interrupted by the dark green of the *colihue* canes.

[22] Coihue: One of the big and beautiful local species of beech trees, the Nothofagus dombeyi.

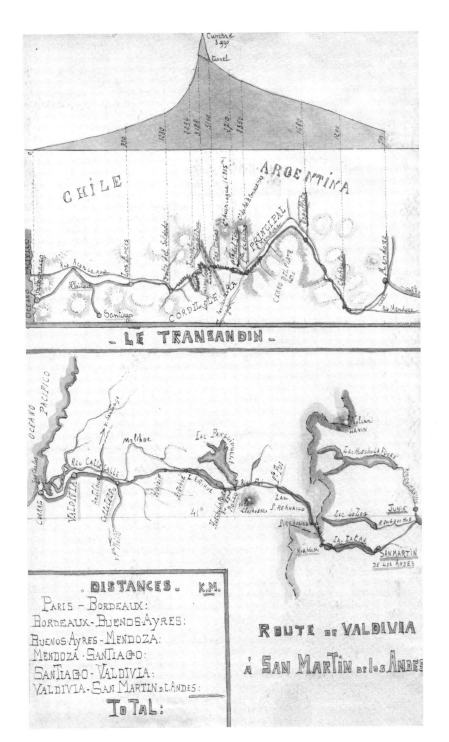

Map of the journey to Valdivia illustrated by don Santiago

At Fuy the ruler was the boss of the ship that crossed the Pire-hueico lake, a gruff character, who emphatically refused to cross them before the scheduled date. The three brothers had to remain there for three days, which were devoted to tourism and canoe paddling, freezing their feet in the snow to later burn their shoes on a salamander with red-hot coals. This salamander was used to cook a detestable meal composed of left over bones boiled with rice, jerked beef tough as a shoe sole, and little more.

Before leaving they took a picture of the captain's wife, who posed on her doorstep straight as a rod, wearing a red shawl and a green dress, with a horrible grimace that was meant to be a smile, a parrot on her shoulder and a child against her knees. The snapshot, once developed, was shocking, although everybody admitted it had been very well taken.

Once the day and the hour had arrived, the captain crossed them in his ship. The numerous turns along the Pirehueico offered time and again new and splendid views. On the other side Ovalle was waiting for them. They had been unable to find him in his home, and he turned out to be a small and cheerful Chilean.

They asked him if he could take them the next day to Huahum; the answer was affirmative, although he had his doubts because of the snow. "Is there a lot of snow?" they asked him. "No, but it has come down a lot these last few days. Now it only reaches up to here." And he pointed to the saddle where the stirrups were fastened.

The young Frenchmen found Pirehueico a charming place, particularly because the uniformity of the forests was cut by small plains bordering the lake. Ovalle had sown some wheat in them, which had not amounted to much, but the three brothers noticed that the fields had not been worked with any intensive method.

Ovalle the Chilean gave them some interesting information concerning the land belonging to the San Martín company. It was one of the best, he said, although it took a lot of snow during harsh winters; it was at the end of the Pirehueico, some twenty thousand hectares, which were on sale at 120.000 pesos. Nine thousand hectares had already been cleared; to the west they reached the Chilean border, north were the Lipinza cliffs, and south the Ipela range. There was no frost in summer, and about three hundred animals could be raised.

That night they slept on beds improvised by their host, and on the following morning they left, guided by Ovalle, who led the way pushing a mule loaded with the luggage. The lake was covered by a thick fog, and the road was not totally bad, because the trail was marked in the snow, which in some places grazed their heels. But before they arrived at the Huahum pass the snow disappeared, and the forest became sparse, interrupted by great plains. There the wind began to blow, bringing with it the news that they were already in the Argentine Patagonia.

When they arrived at Lácar lake they were welcomed by a Dutch family, the Van Dorsers, who pointed to a ship which at that very moment was disappearing in the distance. The captain, without a fixed timetable for the crossings, sailed when he pleased, or simply did not. In this case he had just left, and to expect a speedy return was illusory.

The Dutch provided consolation for this disappointment with a delectable pork cheese, followed by a copious lunch abundantly irrigated with coffee. While the brothers crammed the food to excess, their hosts apologised for having little or nothing to eat, because in fact they had not expected them.

Having decided to carry on their journey come what may, the Larminats engaged a couple of Mapuche indians to take them to San Martín de los Andes in their canoe. This was a comfortable tree trunk carved with an ax and flanked by two outriggers to prevent capsizing. There was no lack of room for the luggage, but progress was slow, in spite of the sail and a good wind from leeward.

The journey was coming to an end, but before arriving they decided to make a stop at *Quechuquina*, Bresler's estate. They did not find the Boer commander in, but his son Ryno was there, a bulky character with shaggy hair, who lived in a *rancho* devoid of light and air, and above all, room. Whoever dared to go in would inevitably stumble in the dark against chests, rocking chairs and the corner of a closet formed by two partitions, which reduced by half the scant space.

The Larminats made an effort to understand the reason for such a troublesome arrangement, in a place where both space and wood for construction were abundant. But they had no choice but to conclude that it must have been a true love for the uncomfortable and the uninhabitable.

In fact there was another explanation, which was given to them by Ryno Bresler as he showed them the installations. A good *estanciero* had to worry above all about having barns, refuges, a corral, a carpentry, all places through which he guided them and which were really well provided. Lodgings, according to this theory, had to be the last of a man's worries. The three brothers assented gravely, but deep inside promised themselves not to imitate him.

The elder Bresler, the Boer commander, had gone to Buenos Aires on business. Soon after they would see another of his sons, Edwin, in San Martín de los Andes. In this town two other children went to school, while a daughter, Corina, was a boarder in a school near Buenos Aires. And the mother? At a certain moment Ryno knocked on a door, from where a rosy-skinned round ball emerged, with a big nose and a sunken mouth, with some strands of hair escaping from a head more or less combed.

She was mama Bresler, who spent all her time locked up in her room, without anybody knowing exactly what she did there.

In spite of their eccentricity, the family showed hospitality, with invitations to stay there as long as they wished, and a restoring lunch of boiled meat and cider (which the brothers decided to start producing as soon as they were able).

But they did not extend their stay. That same afternoon they boarded again the improvised yacht, in which they traveled the last stretch to San Martín de los Andes. It was night when they disembarked half frozen at the pier of the village. Treading on planks no wider than a

FOTO: SANTIAGO DE LARMINAT (1910)

Sailing in a Mapuche canoe

foot, they had to resort to acrobatics to carry luggage and saddles.

Once on land, they discovered that the Company warehouse was closed, but they managed to get in anyway and left the heaviest part of their belongings in a safe place. After this they went to the Ponce Hotel, which surprised them with its comfort. In fact this was only relative, but after their journey they were ready to admire and appreciate a real bed, however modest it chanced to be.

Edwin Bresler joined them for dinner. He looked like a big placid cat, and spoke with extreme slowness. He was his father's exact image, except for the beard, and was just as cunning.

That night, on the beds of the Ponce Hotel, the trip was over. In spite of all the inconvenience it had been instructive, and had finally convinced them of the future of the region, apart from bewildering the three young Frenchmen with its natural beauties.

125

8

The Creation of the Estancia

Don Santiago is front of the Cerro de los Pinos

*T*HE BROTHERS BEGAN WITH THE CONSTRUCTION
of a house, engaging a local carpenter by the name of David
Zumelzu. Meanwhile they rented an estate, *La Avanzada*, two
leagues of land on the margin of the Quemquemtreu, another turbulent sub-tributary of the Limay, where they set up their provisional home. The water of these rivers came down from the Andes
with a tinge of sea-like green, and was the clearest they had ever
seen. The Quemquemtreu flowed at the bottom of a valley laden
with trees on gentle slopes. Firewood was scarce, because the vegetation was made up of some isolated bushes; flora was abundant
only during spring and fall. The most common of the plants that
grew in the high grounds that bordered the valley was the *chacay*,
which resembled a tree by its shape, although in size it was little
more than a bush. The red willow grew by the river. It was the only
big native tree of the region, which seemed predestined to serve as
gazebo for the brindled eagles that abounded in the valley, as well as
dwelling place for the noble ibis and stopping station for vultures
and carrion hawks. The *ñacurutú*, the magnificent big-eared owl,
also visited the willows frequently, and the wildcat, and even the

puma, which used to take a nap lying on the horizontal branches ten or twelve meters from the ground.

The brothers lived in a small dwelling, where they placed three camp beds in a row in the single bedroom and with some planks made a table for the kitchen, which had an excellent oven rented from the Chilean-Argentine Company. During the early days they did their own cooking, which posed no problem, although they disliked having to wash the dishes. But soon they engaged an indian cook, Manuel Islanquin, a spirited man with whom they were very pleased. The food he prepared was tasty, although hardly varied, since the available resources were limited: sheep, carrots, beans, rice, flour, coffee and *chicha*. When they got potatoes, after sending for them and waiting anxiously for their appearance, they were able to add five new dishes to the menu. Bread was provided by the neighbors from *Quemquemtreu*, the same as *chicha*. This drink was a cider made from apples which they had already tasted on their journey, and thought pleasant, to the point of planning to make it at Cerro de los Pinos. In the area there were many wild apple trees, which had multiplied after the first incursions by Jesuit missionaries who came from Chile. The indians killed the Jesuits and destroyed their instruments to till the land, but the seeds they had carried turned into trees, and from the apples produced by those trees, once the juice had fermented, *chicha* was made.

André went to work with the Breslers, at *Quechuquina*, as an apprentice. In spite of the bad impression which this family's lifestyle had made initially, he found the experience of living with them pleasant and useful. In a letter to his family he wrote about the Bresler brothers: "They are two gallant youngsters, very competent regarding everything that concerns farm life, and also excellent teachers. Edwin is a hard worker, all day out in the open, on horseback, driving the cattle from one place to another. Ryno manages the household and looks after the machines and repairs them. I keep going from one to the other, absorbing a great many things. Managing a team of two oxen, I am learning the noble trade of wheat sower. I am beginning to become a horseman; tomorrow we will ride across the whole of the *estancia*, to see falls which they tell me are worth seeing." ·

There were many Mapuche indians in the area, and the Breslers sheltered a tribal chief, a great hunter of *huemuls*, the deer, who had joined the *estancia* to train the dogs which helped in the work. These pure Mapuches were more appreciated than the *criollos*[23], the local farmhands, the Larminats said in their letters, and some of them performed remarkably well. During centuries they had been masters of those regions. Until the middle of the nineteenth century the white man had been unable to conquer the south of Argentina and Chile. One army after the other had failed against their heroic resistance. The clusters of elementary dwellings erected by the white man were always destroyed and burnt by a *malón*[24]; they could only hold on if they were protected by soldiers. It was during the 1880s that general Roca was finally able to subdue them, but anyway, sooner or later the outcome would have been the same. *Mapuches, Tehuelches* and *Araucanos* did not stand a chance against the Remington rifles, or the offer of liquor, and much less before the irrepressible advance of civilization.

Jacques and Etienne, meanwhile, were looking after the sheep that they had bought. They divided them into two flocks, and entrusted each one to a *puestero*[25], whom they paid with money and provisions (five kilos of rice, five of salt and five of *yerba mate*). They soon found the advantages of having *puesteros* working on their own. An income proportional to the wool and the meat that was produced raised the shepherd's interest in his flock.

---

[23] Criollos: This word designated, and still does, the Argentines from the provinces with little or no European blood. As an adjective, it refers to their particular personalities.

[24] Malón: A horde of indians on horseback, assembled to attack white settlers.

[25] Puestero: A laborer, generally married, who is given a house erected in a strategic site on the *estancia*, to work and patrol.

The sheep count was not very good, but better than they had feared. Winter and the lack of care had cost them nine hundred animals. In spite of this they were optimistic, and in their letters they said, with surprise, that lambs were born en masse. They had bought a herd of dapple-gray horses, from a sorrel mother. Needing new ones, they began negotiations with a horse-breaker, who after an expert examination pronounced five of them to be good. "Good" was a horse that could do thirty kilometers in one day without showing fatigue.

That last stretch of winter provided them with excellent weather, when even the wind abated –a strange thing to happen– which seemed in deference to the newcomers. They made use of this to explore the surroundings, rich in volcanoes and remains of all sorts of lava. Game was scarce, only some ducks in the torrents and a few ostriches. In any case, they only had with them their revolvers as the shotguns, with the rest of the luggage, would only arrive at the end of October.

Even though in their letters they boasted being "*Estancieros* in South America", their lifestyles were rudimentary. To begin with they were still on foot, because out of their herd only three horses had been tamed, and these were so thin that it was painful to ride them. So they inspected the *estancia* by walking. But, as spring was imminent, nature had set in motion its metamorphosis, and the rebirth of vegetation was taking place with formidable vigor. The young Frenchmen discovered new forests that they had not seen before, perhaps because the trees had been leafless. "The whole place, so naked fifteen days ago, has been covered as if by magic, and it is a pleasure to see it. Sheep are gaining weight, thanks partly to the shepherds, but mostly because there is abundant grass."

From a present-day perspective, those early steps by my grandfather and his brothers in Patagonia impress as having been tough and requiring great effort. We may be surprised that youngsters brought up enjoying all the comforts offered by civilization could have adapted to such an environment, unknown and destitute. But that was precisely the point; they were young, and driven by the prospect of an enterprise that promised everything, in exchange for long sacrifice. And there was always the charm that lay behind the endless surprises.

One day they attended a grand show: the rodeo of all the horses of the *Quemquemtreu estancia*. Amid tremendous uproar, the farmhands took a herd of horses to the big corral. They saw them approach in a cloud of dust, seven hundred mares, many of them wild, whinnying madly, trying to escape, and pushed towards the gate of the corral by a ring of men armed with whips and lassos.

Once penned, the men worked with them for two days, a task which coincided with a wind storm that raised clouds of thick dust. The horses that were other people's property were returned to their owners, who had shown up when they got news of the rodeo.

Then came the separation of the pregnant mares from the stallions, which was not easy considering that they were untamed animals. The animal that was to be separated was lassoed, and one of the laborers pulled on the lasso while the others, on horseback, pushed the animal from behind.

As a rule the chosen horse had a fixed idea, which was not to go where they wanted to take him, fighting so fiercely that he ended up severing the lasso or bolting desperately until the lasso was taut, finally to fall with a complete somersault.

On the last day the colts were castrated; they were made immobile with a hobble, which was thrown at the front legs while in full race. This difficult operation, called *pialar*, thrilled the farmhands, but frequently hurt the animals when they fell. It required great ability and practice, because the lasso had to be thrown horizontally, close to the ground, in such a way that the horse would step with both legs inside the circle formed by the lasso. At that moment the man would yank it with a quick movement, lowering his body to get a firm stand. As a rule the colt would turn in the air and fall.

FOTO: SANTIAGO DE LARMINAT (1911)

The Cerro de los Pinos in Winter

In October they received the first letters from France, letters which had to travel a long way. The news, the words of encouragement and the recommendations cheered them on to complete the installation at Cerro de los Pinos.

The three brothers began to keep a daily record of the *estancia* in a large copybook. In this copybook they registered the brands of the neighboring *estancias*, made a note of the figures of their business, and recorded the new experiences in their daily life of unskilled *estancieros*. Their pages abound with testimonies of the *criollo* cunning that they fell prey to. Taking advantage of the reputation of naiveté that being newly-arrived Europeans gave them, a Chilean once asked them permission to leave some she-goats in Cerro de los Pinos until they gave birth. Once he got it, he took over not only his goats, but his horses and cattle. Another neighbor, Abdón Fernández, in cahoots with a fence builder called Casanova, sowed wheat and planted potatoes in a far-off site within the *estancia*.

When the brothers reacted against this trespassing, they received all kinds of excuses and delays, but had no other choice than wait until the intruders ended their harvesting.

Dealing with the farmhands was not an easy task either. The brothers worked from dawn till sunset, and it was hard for them to find men able to keep up with their pace. Some of them, rather fussy, resigned after the first observation. Others complained: "Too much work and too little money." Mapuches were as a rule workers in the *estancias* of the region, but with them the problem was the language.

When spring arrived the monotony of the Patagonian plateau began to cheer up with the light green of willow trees, moss and ferns that grew by rapids and cascades, and the wild flowers that abounded in the plains. They were visited by Martrin Donos and La Perrière, who were looking to buy land, but they found that in Bariloche it was poor and expensive, so they went north to try their luck in

135

Misiones. During the visit they discovered La Perrière's talent with the guitar, and they fed their nostalgia singing old French songs.

Jacques worked hard on the organization of the *estancia*. He haggled over the price of wood, indispensable for the house and the furniture, apart from the posts for the fences. He registered before the Justice of the Peace the brands of their flocks, bought cattle, dealt with the counting, the branding and the cures, and kept looking for personnel: a fence builder, the best one to be found, and a foreman. For this position he wrote to the shepherd he had known at Martrin Donos' *estancia*, Gallardo Lavalle, offering him a salary of 190 pesos a month, plus lodging and food. Also on their way were the Ligers, a couple from the region of Sologne engaged by Jean de Larminat who would play an important role in the early years of Cerro de los Pinos.

In spite of their hectic activity, the brothers found time to keep a copious correspondence with their family in France. Jacques and Etienne, fully identified with their status as businessmen, often forgot to include descriptions in their letters which extended over numerous pages on the projects for the *estancia*. André (whose family nickname was "le Wurm", worm in German) wrote to his parents with fun and humor. In one of his letters he wrote in great detail about a visit the three brothers paid to the *Quechuquina estancia* to collect the six thousand pesos that Jacques had loaned Bresler, and to settle the purchase of sheep that Bresler had made for them.

"We went to Quechuquina, where we found all of the Breslers. After breaking the ice that our arrival had produced, they gave us a warm reception; they offered us cartridges, chicken and piglets. Then we talked business, and father Bresler could not have been more polite. To settle the debt all we had to do was take from the *estancia* what we wanted: cows, horses, tools, until arriving at the sum of the six thousand pesos that had been loaned. After talking for a while about the settlement, and only obtaining vague answers, Jacques asked the searing question: —What happened with the extra two thousand pesos that I sent you? —(Surprise) —How much did the sheep cost? —(Long meditation, Bresler rolls his eyes, calculates) —Two fifty —Ah! So they told you they cost two fifty. —Yes, that's what they told me, and that's what I saw in the books. —Ah! They told you... They cost two fifty? Really? —(A long silence, and then, with his best expression as head of the family he unleashed a boisterous and merry laugh:) —Oh, oh, oh! Come along, gentlemen... let us have lunch.— And he introduced us his to little cabin, where the whole family was making an effort to amuse us, to feed us and to give us drink. Corina tried three times to change our napkins, and then went to the piano. They sang the Boer hymn and *La Morocha*[26]. And up to the last moment they were the image of the truest hospitality and goodness. It was touching to see the father, Daniel, observing his small world with moist eyes, playing with a top with his smallest child.

"Next morning, from the moment the sun appeared, work on the estancia went at an infernal pace: Ryno and Edwin with the seeder, Johnnie and Bertie with the pitchforks, the father ordering the farmhands about. Corina dressed up in a costume as a would-be farmer, with a small white bonnet and a skirt with two tucks, feeding the pigeons, while the mother did the washing. We felt ashamed at not doing anything; and furthermore, having come to disturb this patriarchal life with gross considerations about money. In the afternoon relations continued being cordial to the utmost: *chicha*, music, Boer hymn.

"On the morning when we left they appeared really disconsolate, and filled our bags with provisions. The mother said to us: —And above all, if you need anything, if you are ill or wounded, remember that you have a hospital here. And anyway I shall be expecting you for Christmas. —The father could not bear the separation, and shaking our hands time and again said: —Well, friends, may all go well with you! —A sigh, the last goodbye, and we left the place, perfectly indoctrinated us as to the Bresler method."

[26] A very popular song in Argentina at the time.

On December 25 Gallardo Lavalle arrived in the *estancia*, with his clothes and one horse. He would stay there for the rest of his life, working with loyalty and efficiency with the Larminats. Jacques had known him when he was in Olavarría, and his opinion of him did not vary, because he was an excellent foreman. He was not very tall, but fat, *achinado*[27], with a black moustache and bright eyes. He had considerable schooling, wrote well and knew a thing or two about accountancy. He married a woman by the name of Amada, the daughter of a man from the south, Ciriaco Moreno. Their son, Amado Lavalle, also stayed all his life at Cerro de los Pinos and became friend and confidant of the members of the new generation, with whom he discussed every matter, but always steadfastly refusing the post of foreman.

Some days later, already in the new year of 1911, the Ligers arrived; this was another engagement of great importance for the *estancia*. Henri Liger was a sturdy and hard-working man; his rosy skin did not flinch before the tough Patagonian sun, and he undertook in earnest the tasks he was in charge of. He made corrals, constructed sheds, was deft with the scythe, and loved trees as much as the Larminats. He wore a big moustache, which he combed in a way André found amusing, watching how its bright red color varied to a faded gray as grains of the dust driven by the constant wind rested on it. His wife Marie, very diligent, got used without qualms to the lack of comfort, taking upon herself an activity as intense as that of her husband. She was petite but not frail, and meticulous in her chores; in spite of her youth she took a maternal attitude towards the Larminat brothers, who were beginning to miss female company. Marie Liger made life in those early times of austerity a little more convivial and familiar for them.

Moving into Cerro de los Pinos was in the making, although construction of the house was not yet finished. The most difficult part

[27] Achinado: Literally, Chinese-like. It refers to the features of some natives of Argentina, particularly their eyes, sometimes little more than two slits.

On the move

would be crossing the Chimehuin river with the flocks. The long and weary mission took a whole day; it was dark and there were still animals to be crossed. Gallardo opted for driving the sheep where there was more water, and with only two casualties by drowning they reached the shore of round pebbles, on the way to their new home.

Then came the solemn moment when the proprietors moved in. The bags were piled before the front door of the *rancho* at *La Avanzada*, with a column of barrels, a pyramid of sheep hides and the boxes containing their personal effects. They left on the following morning before dawn, a slow-moving train that raised a cloud of dust as it headed towards the hill that separated the two valleys. The afternoon saw them camping on the banks of the Chimehuin. The animals driven by the farmhands followed behind, while foreman Gallardo Lavalle controlled everything seated in his black sheepskin saddle. Henri Liger, inside the house, was completing the preparations. The

139

river Jordan, if it had not parted its waters, at least had now lowered them somewhat to allow the crossing, and on the next day, "God willing", they would be able to enter the Promised Land.

And so it happened, but their arrival did not imply an end to their problems. To begin with, they had to evict another intruder in the house, together with his wife, who had even sown some crops in the fields. This man had acted in league with the fence builder, who had assured him that the French were "good people"; they were rich, they ignored the ways of the country, and it was always possible to come to terms with them. Jacques, who was already earning a reputation as the most determined of the brothers, faced the trespasser and scared him as was necessary to make him flee. After this episode they had to negotiate with the carpenter, who was deliberately delaying the end of the work, because he felt very comfortable occupying the house. They also got rid of him.

Another problem, more difficult to deal with, was the existence of the "southern route" that crossed the estate. This meant large herds of about a thousand oxen, cows and horses going through about three times a week. During this action it often happened that they took cattle from the *estancia*, an accident which the herd drivers claimed was no fault of theirs, because those animals happened to be in the way and they just joined the march of their own free will. Another problem was the gigantic clouds of dust that the marching herds raised.

All in all, moving in filled the brothers with joy, although the operation was not yet complete. The cart that they had engaged to carry the load from the house arrived at *La Avanzada,* one day late. Jacques and Etienne shortened the waiting by weighing and loading the boxes. This was no minor job, especially considering the box that contained the linen from the big Parisian store Le Bon Marché, which weighed one hundred and-fifty three kilos. At last, after gathering the oxen that had scattered, the cart got moving, and the first load departed en route to Cerro de los Pinos. Meanwhile Jacques went out to have a look. What happened next was the substance of a letter he wrote that same evening to his father.

"It is eight p.m. Ah! My old man! Catastrophe! But let us proceed by stages. The moment I arrived at the hill from where I was to control the operation with my binoculars, aimed at Cerro de los Pinos and other prominent points, I heard a tremendous clattering noise: kaboom!, coming from the other side of the crest of the hill. I moved forward, nothing. Dead silence... no cloud of dust. I advanced a little more, and in a small dale I spotted the cart, overturned and lying on one side, while a cascade of barrels, boxes, sacks, theodolites and everything else rolled towards the Chimehuin. It may be that I am exaggerating because the cart, instead of falling towards the valley, overturning on the slope, fell towards the hill, surely due to a very skillful maneuver, so the damage could have been much worse. All in all disaster is reduced to two camp beds broken in bits, ten cans of biscuits that lost their bottoms, and some boxes that did not contain anything fragile. It is nothing. Having to load again two thousand kilos of things is no chicken feed, as it is said. The cart driver, with Oriental calm, let the oxen loose, remaining unruffled, and started to untie the load. He appeared to be very ashamed because I had witnessed his accident. But this did not prevent him from telling me that he could not have managed alone. We barely have time, before sunset, to unload, arrange things, put the cart straight and load it again. I should have procured a steam crane! We have dispatched the last load. We are, at last, about to take possession of our house, which closes an era and opens another."

The Trip to Magellan's Strait

La Hardonnière

TWO YEARS HAD ELAPSED SINCE JACQUES BOARDED ship in Bordeaux to set off on the Argentine adventure, and the achievements up to then were enough to make him proud. Although everything was still in the making, he had already found a place which fitted his dreams, had made it his, and had begun its transformation into a prosperous enterprise. Having reached that point, and in accordance with what had previously been agreed upon with his family, it was time to return to France to visit his kin. Jacques was longing to see his parents again, and his brothers and sisters, to report in his own voice the many experiences he had gone through, as well as anxious to tell his father about his ideas and projects. In those times a father's word was law, but experience had matured young Jacques; and, one of his traits had been always to break established rules.

On May 5, 1911, he left Buenos Aires, for a France that awaited him in full spring. La Hardonnière was blooming more than ever. The meeting was warm, and he felt comfortable surrounded by the love of his family and of his friends. He was particularly happy to renew his visits to the neighboring château de la Turpinière, owned by the large de Maindreville family, with whom the Larminats had always been very close. Among the many children who took part in the merry holiday gatherings was little Magdelon, who listened with curiosity to the stories of that world which appeared before her eyes so distant and inhospitable. Surely she must have been impressed by the exotic and different appearance that Jacques had acquired: for the little French girl who years later would make all those stories her own, he was already an American.

To his surprise, Jacques found that he could not drive Cerro de los Pinos out of his mind; but his nostalgia was practical and busy. He collected oak and beech seeds with the hope of adapting those trees to Patagonia; he visited neighboring estates looking for the best Rambouillet rams, and kept on the lookout for modern machinery to take back with him.

He had long talks with his father, telling him everything about the *estancia*; he drew caricatures of laborers and neighbors to illustrate anecdotes that reflected the wide cultural differences, and the clashes that those differences implied. In objective terms, the site where he had settled in South America was a desert, a forlorn land where only foreign colonizers dared to settle, and served as a refuge to criminals and fugitives who took advantage of the isolation and interminable distances. But in his descriptions it was a paradise with mountains covered with forests of fascinating species, abounding in land almost unexplored, which had everything to put the cattle breeder or the farmer on the way to wealth, with additional possibilities to forest the empty territory which was improved by the sediment of volcanic ashes. Everything was waiting to be done, and the challenge to transform that barrenness into an orchard outlined the perspective of a future that was worth experiencing. The latter became more evident when contrasted with the situation in Europe, where war clouds loomed.

Two years before, when Jacques was leaving France, confidential information about the potencial outbreak of war had circulated with growing insistence in all of Europe, but particularly in the countries of the "Entente" (France and England) and its rival, Germany.

Jacques read the newspapers and perceived the numerous incidents that announced the Great War, but half his heart was elsewhere, and he was interested as much or even more in the news he received from Patagonia. A letter from his brothers informed him of the hazardous arrival of Gallardo Lavalle, who had established himself at the *estancia* with his family.

Travelling on a huge cart painted blue and red, christened with the poetic name of "The Light of Hope", Lavalle had managed to cross the first branch of the Chimehuin, but in spite of the spirited efforts of Poroto and Lista, the two mild oxen of the *estancia*, aided by a dozen horses, Gallardo was unable to cross the second branch of the river. The whole family had to fall back to the island, where they camped during the night. They tried again on the following day and succeeded, pulled by three yokes of oxen and four horses. Seen from the civilized countryside of La Hardonnière this story seemed from another time, primitive and heroic. So Jacques felt, perhaps for the first time, but instead of discouraging him it filled him with zest by allowing him to measure once more the scope of the challenge he had undertaken.

In November, with the first frosts of northern winter, he boarded ship back to Argentina, loaded with letters and presents for his brothers, arriving in time to celebrate Christmas at Cerro de los Pinos.

Calm did not last long, because in the first days of 1912 Martrin Donos and Roberto Iselin visited the *estancia*, on a reconnaissance trip south ("south of south"), and invited Jacques to join them. They did not have to insist, because for him adventure and the unknown were always tempting. The trip was made, and it was a high point in my grandfather's life, as he rode over two thousand kilometers on horseback and five hundred kilometers by coach, collected first hand valuable information about all of Patagonia, experienced unforgettable stories, and painted his best watercolors.

They chose nineteen saddle horses and two packhorses for the trip. Jacques took with him a troop of bays, with a newborn mare, and mounted his piebald Curupio. Martrin Donos took his own chestnut-colored horse, and also contributed a stupendous herd from his *estancia La Totora*. Iselin bought a mule and two horses from a Chilean for the occasion.

They departed on one of those beautiful Patagonian dawns which happen on the rare occasions when there is no wind. As they rode away they could hear the faint sounds coming from the *estancia*: the bleating of sheep, the barking of dogs and the farmhands' shouts. The calmness of the clear morning brought other sounds from the neighboring dales. They went a long way by the wide "road to Chile", the rustlers' path, opened by the hoofs of hundreds of thousands of cattle taken by the indian *malones* in the Argentine pampas before they were defeated in "the conquest of the desert", as it was named by the Argentine government and press. At the time, a series of bartering operations sent that cattle to be fattened in the great alfalfa tracts of the big Chilean *estancieros*, some of whom were pinpointed as financing the incursions by the indians. The road bordered the varied winding of the Limay river along the bottom of the valley, the water lapping the dry and craggy slopes.

The first awakening of the excursion was catastrophic. The magnificent horses from *La Totora*, poorly tamed, had disappeared, ignoring their lead mare. The packhorse rebelled and threw off the parcels it was loaded with, scattering them. Iselin's two Chilean horses had also gone, and their owner had to find them and rope them, an operation he had to repeat every morning that the trip lasted. However, the good humor and disposition of the friends overcame the obstacles.

Jacques was pressed to get to the Nahuel Huapi region, which he did not know yet and which had been praised for its beauty. An area of splendid forests, the native indians considered it a paradise before the arrival of the white man, and they were not mistaken. The perfume of wild strawberries filled the air with a particular scent, overriding the harshness of the altitude in the high Andes. Amid the foliage of trees and elegant ferns, clusters of geraniums appeared here and there, together with the brilliantly colored *calceolarias* and *adesmias* bordering the rushes. Erosion by mountain waters had carved splendid gullies that extended up to the high arid hills in the center of the territory. The grass growing in that area reached up to a meter and a half and some magnificent animals could be found. The travelers saw in those almost uninhabited valleys horses of surprising proportions and beauty.

Upon arrival at Nahuel Huapi they stopped at the *Tequel Malal estancia*, belonging to Juan Jones, a pioneer in the use of fences who had established himself by the lake in 1889, after working as a herd driver in Chaco and in Buenos Aires. With a reputation for hospitality, he had invited Ramón Lista and the topographical expert Francisco Moreno as guests, supplying the latter free of charge with a herd of horses for the (Chile) Border Commission. Jacques was interested in the stories about Moreno, particularly the one about the time when he was a captive of the Saihueque indians in their camp in Caleufu, in 1880, from where he escaped in a raft along the Limay. All that sounded remote, and yet it was clear that Patagonia had changed little in the quarter of a century since the end of Roca's campaign.

Leaving behind the few *estancias* around lake Nahuel Huapi, they began a series of long marches following the deserted valley, where the only sound was the shrieks of lapwings and the murmur of the wind shaking the clumps of stiff straw or the languid willow branches. In five days they saw very few herdsmen. They were surprised by the unfriendliness of these people, who hardly spoke to them, even when they unsaddled in the same place to shelter from the sun, and shared company for many hours. They noticed that each of these men prepared his own *maté*, without offering it to the others; the solitary nature of the Patagonian dweller, aggravated by distrust, had changed the sociable rite of taking *maté*. It was a common occurrence in those times that many inhabitants of Patagonia had no identity papers, since often their emigration to those regions had been forced by accounts pending with the law. This did not necessarily give rise to fear, but it was a fact that many horse thieves and bandits had their hideouts in the vast regions of Chubut and Santa Cruz, where they were able to move at ease thanks to limited policing and the isolation of the inhabitants.

The best known of these refugees had been Asencio Brunel, who fled to Patagonia after committing murder. For some years he was busy with the theft of animals, especially horses, and was known to drive away huge herds and then choose the best animals at his leisure, which allowed him to escape at a gallop to commit another outrage in a distant place. His mere presence was enough to fill his victims with fear: he had a dreadful aspect, dirty, in tatters, his body was covered with thongs of puma skin, all of which contrasted with a remarkable horsemanship and an intimidating eye. He was accused of the murder of the Patagonian *estanciero* Máximo Formel, and newspapers demanded that the bandit whom they called "the terror of *estancieros*" be captured. He was, several times, and always managed to flee, mocking fetters, pillories and the severest guards. Until the Tehuelche indians from chief Kankel's camp, fed up with the many thefts of their horses, picked up his trail, found him, and summarily executed him. For a long time people claimed seeing the likes of Brunel on a hill, his hair disheveled and the puma skins fluttering wildly in the Patagonian wind.

During his journey south Jacques did not see better land than the one he had bought at Cerro de los Pinos. In fact, he never had cause to feel sorry about his decision. With the exception of Bariloche, where land was slightly dearer, aridity was rampant. Chubut seemed an immense desert, savannas of rock with bushes that were always dying, and a monotonous landscape with no variations of flora or fauna. Only guanacos were seen now and then, and flocks of ostriches, which upon seeing the horsemen fled dodging shrubs and clumps of tall grass. The *chulengos*[28] had a mediocre flesh for the taste of the travelers, and grown up guanacos were too difficult to catch. These

Tehuelches

animals semed to designate one of the males to act as lookout, and with its cry of alert, a sort of whinny more like a big laugh, warned the flock to escape. *Choiques*, the young ostriches, were a bit slower, and a doubly coveted prey, for the meat, especially the sirloin and kidney, and for the hide, which made superb quilts. Jacques record-ed in his diary the immense flocks of guanacos that they saw, always from a distance, in the deserted regions of the south of Chubut; extremely shy, these animals escaped to the areas where the soil was rockier, where they knew that they could not be caught.

Due to the heat the travelers preferred to travel by night, guided by the Southern Cross. They had taken with them the only trust-worthy map of the region that existed at that time, the one drawn by

[28] Chulengos: Young guanacos

151

Edward VII's Commission, responsible for arbitration in the border dispute between Chile and Argentina.

In June 1899 Francisco Pascasio Moreno had shared with the Royal Society in London some thoughts which were still valid: "We talk about aridity, about deserts, about difficulties for communications, and we do not ask ourselves if countries with greater obstacles did not achieve progress. I do not think that I am a visionary if I prophesy an abundant population in the provinces of the interior. As for the Patagonian territories, marvels can be performed there." And a little before the trip made by Jacques and his friends, in 1909, Moreno had written in an article in the newspaper *La Nación*: "The Argentine map, in what concerns that part of our territory, is at present a blank just as it was when I crossed it in 1879".

Several years before Moreno arrived in the region, a Frenchman had tried to settle in this part of the northern Patagonia, following a romantic dream.

His name was Orélie Antoine de Tounens, and he was born in Chourgnac, near Périgueux. He was an attorney at law having completed his degree in Toulouse university, and he had started a law firm in Périgueux which was not successful.

Tounens then sought to be crowned King of Patagonia by the Araucanian tribes that were restless in southern Chile. He thought that the indians would revolt against the Chilean government which wanted to control the whole of Patagonia.

He moved to Buenos Aires in 1852 and later to Santiago de Chile and then to Concepción where he started conversations with the mightiest *caciques* of the region like Quilapán and Calfucura. At first, he succeeded and was crowned King of Araucania and Patagonia by a large assembly of Mapuche tribes gathered in the valley of Los Angeles.

Orélie-Antoine I and his allies founded the kingdom of Araucania and Patagonia on November 17, 1860. It was a constitutional and hereditary monarchy. The Constitution was modern and democratic because Tounens was an honest and well intentioned man. He created the Royal Council, Ministries, even a Parliament elected by universal suffrage, and a State Council. The territory had the rivers Bío-Bío in Chile, and the rivers Neuquén and Negro in Argentina as its northern limit, and it included all the lands located to the south of such rivers, between the Atlantic and Pacific Oceans, including Tierra del Fuego.

The King issued money and coins, named the members of the Royal Council that were chosen from among his friends, the Araucanian *caciques*, had a national anthem written and created a green, white and blue national flag.

In 1862, the king, Orélie-Antoine I, was kidnapped by a Chilean patrol and taken to court in an unlawful manner. He was thrown into jail in Los Angeles, and then in Santiago, and the Chilean government finally sent him back to France trying not to create a problem with the French empire. Napoléon III never took De Tounens seriously and he eventually died in poverty in Tourtoirac in 1886.

My grandfather said that it was lucky that France didn't try to back De Tounens officially, because he would probably have been abandoned in the middle of the adventure as was Maximilian in Mexico. On that occasion, Napoléon III called Bazaine back to France with the well known tragic consequences for the emperor Maximilian and his followers. Mygrandfather always said that France didn't have neither enough interest nor enough knowledge to be a prominently ranked partner for Latin American countries.

Strangely enough, the Kingdom of Araucania and Patagonia still exists "in exile" and it has a considerable number of fans across the world, united in clubs or other institutions. There is even a Royal Heir, a Consul General and there are nobility titles.

In the years 1984 and 1998, a group of commandos supporting the kingdom occupied an islet in the Jersey Islands and raised the green, white and blue flag in order to "take revenge" for the aggression committed by England against the Kingdom when British troops retook the Malvinas in 1982.

In spite of the cartographic precariousness, Jacques was able to direct his friends, after four days of night marches, to Putrachoique, the only point on the map. It was a desert forgotten by Argentines, into which almost nobody ventured, with the exception of scientists such as D'Orbigny, Darwin and Moreno, who had good reason to congratulate themselves for their daring when they discovered its geological riches, well preserved fossils and prehistoric paintings.

Jacques was also fascinated by the evidence of the great geological phenomena that had left their trail in Patagonia. A born geologist, he was interested in the variety of rocks he found by the rivers, the granite fragments, basalt and trachyte of different colors dragged as alluvium, in which a story of millenniums could be read. Little by little facts were adding up to complete his Patagonian bewitchment.

Used to the European scale, where geography was predictable and each detail had been described and catalogued since ancient times, in Patagonia everything was unknown, everything was waiting to be discovered. In a way that was exciting; in another, it was baffling. Plateaus without roads and full of rocks hampered progress, horses went lame easily, and the meager pasturelands weakened them day by day. The gnarled slopes where only the winding paths of guanacos could be seen made descent by horses very difficult, either due to the lack of practice of the three travelers, or the fear of the animals which never looked away from the yawning depths that they were made to circle. The packhorse had to be blindfolded, after once having bolted, spreading bundles all over the place. Rivers could be simple puddles of mud which served as home to a few bald coots, or neat courses of water where enormous trout could be fished or even rushes with vortexes of foam, which were very difficult to cross. As a rule in the vicinity of rivers and lakes the landscape changed abruptly; dryness was replaced by sprawling green grasslands, irrigated by fountains where wild watercress grew, and the dark leaves of *calafate*[29] appeared. Fresh

[29] Calafate: A small shrub of southernmost Patagonia, which yields a red fruit used to make jam.

water and saline lakes abounded in the plateaus. This compensated for the aridity of the soil but there the mosquitoes multiplied; attacking the travelers in the heat of the afternoon: nothing seemed capable of stopping the insects, not even the sudden changes in temperature of the Patagonian summer, that can reach thirty degrees Celsius difference between day and night.

Among the high grass lived the straw cat, a fiend of small proportions but ferocious with its victims, rodents and small lambs. This cat defended itself courageously, and was very difficult to hunt. And there was the puma, which fed on guanacos, but could also attack horses. This animal, which had caused ignorant travelers so many worries, never attacked man, whom it feared, and with whom it could even become friendly.

Félix de Azara's anecdote from the times of the viceroyalty was well-known; during four months this man had kept a puma cub that enjoyed playing with the slaves and purred under caresses. The countryman respected it in the desert, considering it a shy animal with little intelligence, but did not tolerate its attacking his own animals, especially because in one night with a "playful attitude" it was capable of killing sixty goats or the same number of sheep. In those cases the countryman would kill it without hesitation. The puma resigned itself to becoming extinct at the hands of man, whom it flatly refused to consider an enemy. However, if the hunter was accompanied by dogs, the puma became a daring and vicious animal.

Before arriving in the populated area of Santa Cruz, Jacques, Iselin and Martrin Donos were left without provisions and had to feed on guanacos and armadillos, and when these were lacking, on the scarce rice that they still had. Further on, during a long stretch, and when absolutely all provisions were gone, they did not find a thing to hunt or fish for several days. Hunger made them consider killing one of the horses, or chewing the girths, but the situation changed completely when they reached the *estancias* in the region of lakes San Martín, Viedma and Argentino. Here they were greeted with unsparing meals, which ended up unbalancing their punished stomachs. A rest became imperative, which they used to make some useful observations of the surroundings.

The province of Santa Cruz was only suitable to raise sheep, and land cost no more than five pesos the hectare. The plateaus and glacial valleys, with the wind permanently hitting the plains, could not be compared with the beautiful landscapes of Neuquén.

A curious character they found there was Juan de Liniers, Count of Buenos Aires, great-grandson of Santiago de Liniers, hero of the defense and reconquest of Buenos Aires, in 1806 and 1807. As a reward for his action during those British invasions, Santiago de Liniers was named viceroy and was granted the title of Count of Buenos Aires by the Spanish Crown, only to be shot for spying for the King a little after the May 1810 Revolution, having previously fled with the viceroyalt's treasury. This descendant had little in common with his illustrious ancestor; knowing that the French travelers were approaching, Juan de Liniers rode out to meet and greet them, standing on his horse on one foot and waving in the air a bottle of excellent cognac.

They also visited another French family in Santa Cruz, the Bonvalets, who told them truculent stories of that region, where the arm of the law arrived weak and without much conviction. Some time before, during the Sáenz Peña presidency, the Frontier Police had been created, almost as a "Foreign Legion" because it was made up of men from different origins and nationalities, with backgrounds of uneven character. They were expert horsemen, skilled in the handling of saber and carbine, and merciless with their captives. The paramount mission of this corps was to control the proliferation of bandits in Patagonia. Their most famous action had been the persecution of the outlaws Wilson and Evans, who had settled near Esquel trading in cattle, a business which they expanded with robbery. Their nemesis was the holdup of the Compañía Mercantil in Arroyo Pescado, where they assassinated an engineer, Llwyd Ap Iwan, a prominent member of the

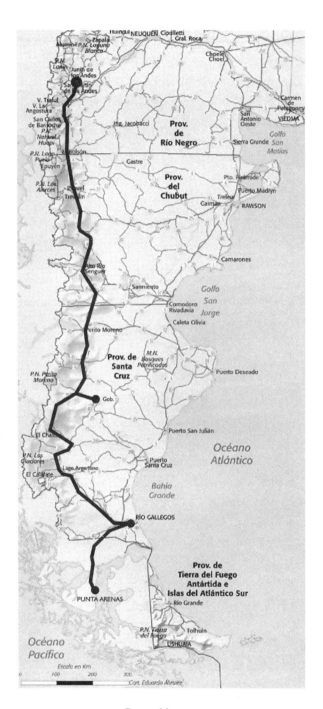

Route Map

Welsh community. Ap Iwan had performed valuable work as a geographer and explorer, resulting in the discovery of the Fénix river in Santa Cruz, a fact which served to confirm the arguments put forward by Moreno in the conflict over the limits with Chile. This crime exhausted the tolerance of the authorities. The Frontier Police went after Wilson and Evans for a whole year, fighting gun battles on four occasions, without being able to finish them off. Finally, as a consequence of a kidnapping they were located by the Frontier Police, and after a bloody battle both bandits were killed.

The harassing of the Chilean bandits that crossed the boundary lines resulted in the capture of José Pozzi, a highwayman who inspired terror for the ferocity of his crimes. But many men who had scores to settle with the law escaped from urban zones and joined the Frontier Police, where they became excellent agents, of great valor and efficiency.

The travelers also enjoyed the experience of a compatriot, Jean de Reille, who raced against the police commissioner on horseback and let him win out of convenience. They attended an elegant dinner at the *estancia* of Baron Lascazes, but they thought that the Baroness didn't look one of her rank at all.

Having finally recovered, Jacques and his two friends abandoned the comfort of the *estancias* surrounding the lakes and set off across the wide plains of Santa Cruz, which in spite of their gray uniformity held surprises that charmed them. On the verge of the rivers Santa Cruz and Gallegos, whose valleys were covered with stunted trees and thick underbrush, they found numerous guanaco cemeteries. All guanacos from the surrounding plains went to those sites when they felt the time for death was approaching. This animal, a relative of the camel, of gregarious habits, which survived and prospered in places where any other herbivorous animal would die of starvation, complied with this ultimate pilgrimage following the voice of a mysterious instinct.

They found a native indian funerary cairn on top of a cliff: a pile of rocks and dried branches, where bones whitened by time could be seen through its openings. When the Tehuelche indians reigned in the southern pampas, they buried their dead on the highest points of the plains. When the white explorers appeared, they were forced to conduct their burials at less exposed sites. The Tehuelche funerary rites demanded that the weapons he had used be buried with the dead man; his horses were slaughtered and on the day following his death some objects that had belonged to him were also buried. The dead man would need his lasso, his knife and his horse to hunt in the fertile fields that extended beyond the "big water" (the sea) where guanacos and ostriches abounded.

The three young Frenchmen met with the native indians. The horses that Martin Donos had contributed to the expedition had not become used to the toughness of the *coirón* grass, and bad nourishment rendered them useless, so they had to resort to Tehuelche indians to buy horses that would allow them to continue. The Tehuelche camp was located about a hundred kilometers north of the Santa Cruz river. The natives had selected a deep and sheltered valley, with good grass and even better fountainheads. About fifty wild horses, the pride of the chief of the region, grazed there. These animals were the survivors of old flocks which for ages had roamed the pampas. Their ancestors had been the horses brought by the colonizers, and at the end of several centuries of freedom and abundant grass, became the natives' most efficient weapon; their resistance enabled them to gallop for several leagues without tiring. It was from this biological background that Solanet, after long expeditions to the end of Patagonia in search of the animals with the least contaminated blood, obtained the samples with which he created the *Criollo* race, a miracle of adaptation recognized the world over.

Negotiations with the Tehuelches proved harder than had been expected, and reaching an agreement took several days. During that period Jacques made observations about the life and habits of these peaceful people. He tried to find arrow carvers, of whose work he had seen perfect samples in the funerary mounds, but constant contact with the white man, and the uselessness of arrows against firearms, had made them lose that primitive craft.

Jacques had to content himself with buying some guanaco and skunk skins, while his friends opted for foxes and seals. He also bought some elegant silver bracelets made with *patacones*[30], which years later would be part of the trousseau of his fiancée Magdelon.

With fresh horses they carried on galloping south, accompanied, when not propelled, by a wind which thwarted speech and breathing. The four leagues that they rode up the sinister valley of the Tucutuco river exhausted the horses. The rodents that had given their name to the river had potholed the soil in such a way that every other step the horses would sink up to their knees.

The southern wind unleashed all its fury, bringing a hailstorm with it. The thermometer descended to zero degrees Celsius and further ahead the travelers were enveloped in sleet that obliterated all vision. Inevitably they lost their course, and Jacques noticed that Iselin was lagging behind, shouting being of no use, because the wind shouted louder.

There was a risk of losing the packhorse, which was carrying the scant provisions they had left, together with the tinder box and the ponchos they had in case bad weather persisted. To lose horse and garments in such a situation could prove fatal, while the snow made things worse, since it erased trails, moistened the matches, hampered eyesight, burnt boots and stiffened bodies.

Jacques recalled some advice given to him by experienced *paisanos*[31], which turned out to be very useful on this occasion.

"If you find it is night and you have lost your way, the thing to do is to feel the inclination of the bushes. In Patagonia they are always leaning west to east, due to the wind. If you must sleep in the open it is better not to undress, because if you have to get up in haste the wind will not blow your clothes away. Matches and a flint must

[30] Patacones: An old silver coin weighing one ounce, Argentine monetary unit in the nineteenth century.
[31] Paisanos: farm workers, natives of a region.

160

Journey to Magellan. Second morning, departure

1911. A solitary man walks with his compass counting his paces.
Andrés draws the map of the property

May 25. ¡"Viva la Patria"!

Winter at Cerro de los Pinos

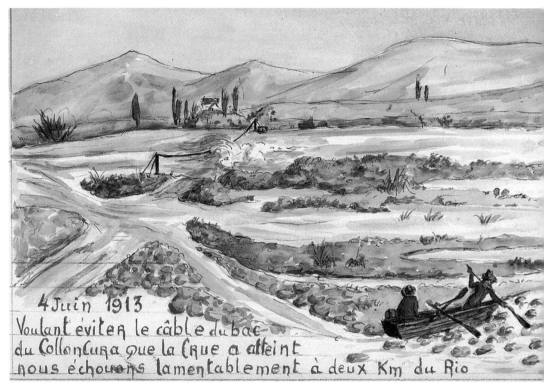

4 Juin 1913
Voulant éviter le câble du bac
du CollonCura que la Crue a atteint
nous échouons lamentablement à deux Km du Rio

June 4, 1913. Trying to avoid a cable in the water from the Collón Cura ferry,
we run aground two kilometres away from the river

2 Juin 1913. LA BARRE DU LIMAY.

June 2, 1913. The Limay Barra

*1914. My great grandfather Jean de Larminat and his seven sons
who enlisted in the First World War*

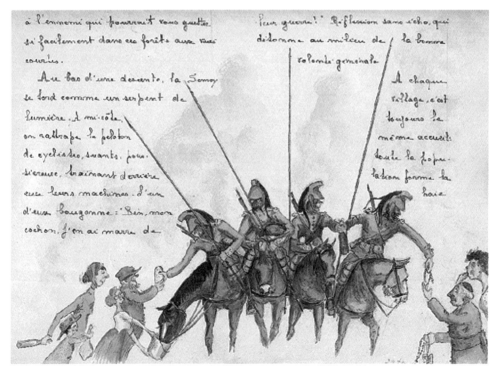

July, 1914. The Dragoons organize to receive presents from the people

June, 1918. Germans in the darkness reach the Parroy woods, while Jacques and his patrol await them at Sanon bridge

July 19 and 20, 1918. Armoured battle.
"My Lieutenant", says Lombard to Jacques, "the whole lot are dead"

October, 1915. Jacques is evacuated wounded

September, 1915. In single file we go through a devastated landscape

April, 1920. Don Roberto inspects the building of Jacques's home on the south shore of the Chimehuín river

April 28, 1920. Wedding trip. Jacques and Magdelon arrive at Cerro de los Pinos

1920. The loyal foreman Gallardo Lavalle is decorated with the medal of "French Merit"

1920. First night at the new house. Night watch. Don Santiago and Magdelon

1924. Fiesta at the "estancia"

1940. Castrating

1947. Feast at the end of castrating

1949. Don Esteban takes the wool from the river's north shore to the south

December, 1954. Herds driven to the summer pastures "La Veranada" del Pato

December, 1954. First herd. Five thousand sheep arrive at the new estancia
"La Nicolasa" in Chimpay

Société Rurale
du Neuquen
Junin de los Andes
1955: André présente à la Vente notre Grand Champion.

*1955. Don Andrés shows his Australian Merino Grand Champion for sale
at the Rural Society in Neuquén*

1959. Taming with spectators and picnic

July, 1953. The flooding of the river in the first winter of the Black Bridge

1966. The fonnders rest. Don Santiago (77) and Don Esteban (82)

always be carried. In winter, the flight of the great bustard indicates direction; he always flies southeast to migrate. The dog is good company, because it helps when hunting and drives away harmful animals like the fox, which although it does not attack humans, it has the vicious habit of chewing the horses' headgear. More than one rider has been left horseless because of this." And above all, Jacques recalled Gallardo Lavalle's advice at parting: "Beware, boss, of the knocks that Patagonia gives."

Under the lee of a rock and by a fire, wrapped up in the skins bought from the Tehuelches, the three travelers spent that stormy night. On the following morning they resumed their march.

After crossing the last lap of the high Patagonian plateau, they arrived at the settlements around Punta Arenas, a Chilean township spread over an elevation facing the Strait of Magellan. They had thus arrived at the end of their journey, which had demanded almost three months.

For their return they boarded the *Camarones*, a ship of the German company Hamburg-Süd, and during a call al the Gallegos river Jacques wrote to his father: "I am delighted to have made this trip, which has enabled me to find new perspectives for the sale of wool. I am returning with the impression that the Andes offer many excellent centers, but that ours is one of the best. We have seen fine land, forests and pampas, areas where grass reached our knees and others with foul weeds to no end, plus splendid and unforgettable scenery. It is difficult to imagine a more diversified region than this mountain range. But, oh, how much more I prefer our life in Neuquén, cheered by its apple trees, its cows and its agriculture. This trip has given me the resolution to buy more land where we are now, and I plan to see to that immediately. I have decided to pay up to twenty pesos the hectare."

The boat left Jacques in Buenos Aires, where he secured provisions for the winter in Cerro de los Pinos. His shopping list gives an idea of what life on the *estancia* and its menu were like: five hundred kilos of rice, four hundred and fifty of *yerba maté*, a hundred of dry beans, five hundred of sugar, and two hundred liters of petrol. Quantities may seem excessive, but they show the difficulties involved in replacing supplies in the south.

Jacques did the last lap from Neuquén to the *estancia* in the rickety wagon that took the mail to the Andes every eight days. Seated as best he could in the angular coachman's seat, he had to put up with the cutting wind and the exasperating slowness of the mules, which moved across the sandy plains at no more than three kilometers an hour, when not altogether brought to a stop because of some hindrance in the terrain. When his patience came to an end he got off and walked twenty kilometers in one go up to the nearest post, the township of Arroyitos. Here he bought a saddled horse, with which he was able to carry on.

After a long day's ride across the rugged fields of the Chocón, Jacques unsaddled, lit a fire, and after cooking himself a barbecue fell sound asleep. A disagreeable surprise awaited him at dawn, as he woke up. The horse had returned to its owner. So Jacques had no choice but to wait for the coach. When it arrived his ill humor took another twist as the coachman told him that he had seen that horse being sold on about fourteen previous occasions, always leaving its rider on foot. The only consolation that Jacques had was the saddle, an unpleasant memento of local cunning, with which Jacques was already becaming familiar.

The War

Don Santiago de Larminat, 1918

Silencio en la noche... Ya todo está en calma...
El músculo duerme... La ambición descansa...
Un clarín se oye... Peligra la Patria...
Y al grito de guerra los hombres se matan
Cubriendo de sangre los campos de Francia...

TANGO DE GARDEL, LE PERA AND PETTOROSSI[32]

O SOONER HAD HE RETURNED TO CERRO de los Pinos than –according to the decision he had made on his journey– Jacques began negotiations with the Chilean-Argentine Company to buy the extra land to complete the definitive extension of the *estancia*. The deal was agreed in mid-May. The Larminat brothers celebrated the acquisition of eleven thousand hectares to complete the six plots of the cadastre south of the Chimehuin river. André, compass in hand, counting his paces in the solitude of Patagonia, established the final boundary of the total fifteen thousand hectares, later drawing such a perfect map that his uncle Etienne had it printed by the Topographic Society in Paris.

The three Larminats already felt attached to this land by bonds of belonging; it had proved to be not so inhospitable, and they were

---

[32] *"The night is silent... all is quiet...*
"The musician sleeps... ambition is at rest...
"A bugle is heard... the country is in danger...
"And at the call of war men kill each other
"Covering with blood the fields of France...

Tango by Gardel, Le Pera and Pettorossi

leaving their imprint on it. Among the traditions that they began to observe, one was that every May 25[33] it rained, a fact that did not prevent the patriotic celebrations, and much less the dancing, in which the *criollos* participated with their particular tap dances, even if they had mud up to their knees. Snow arrived in July, and in September the animals gave birth, a month of work that the flocks demanded. The pleasures of spring and the fury of the wind continued to surprise them, and, overcoming difficulties, they were able to get the first trees to grow, which became emaciated shelters close to the houses. The Ligers, indefatigable workers, had a good chance to show their mettle in summer, when the kitchen garden and the fruit trees were at their best. To this don Henri Liger added the harvesting of wheat, a matter in which, surpassing his bosses in practical knowledge, he taught them to perform.

During 1912 the electoral reform promoted by president Roque Sáenz Peña was consolidated, and established that voting was to be secret and compulsory for all citizens. This was a most significant step towards the building of democracy in Argentina. Public opinion welcomed the projects concerning electoral reform, and in the parliamentary elections in April of that year the Radical Civic Union won in the city of Buenos Aires and in the province of Santa Fe. Apart from this, two socialists, Juan B. Justo and Alfredo Palacios, plus two independent candidates obtained seats in Congress. The Radical leader, Hipólito Yrigoyen, who until then had been preaching abstention, had to admit the fairness of the new method, which would carry him to the presidency in 1916.

Buenos Aires was growing in population and works. Construction started on the *Diagonal Sud*, downtown, and the Lacroze company was authorized to build an underground. However, conflicts arose in the interior. In June 1912 the ruinous situation of many lessees of land, most of them immigrants, gave rise to a strike known

---

[33] May 25: Anniversary of the first home rule in Argentina.

as *"El Grito de Alcorta"*, Alcorta's call, which spread across cereal-growing areas, especially south of Santa Fe, southeast of Córdoba, north of the province of Buenos Aires, Entre Ríos and La Pampa. This protest reflected the conflicts that agriculture in the pampas generated. Lessees, day laborers, store owners and big landlords coexisted with different and contradictory interests.

After a year of drought and another in which the price of maize dropped, the lessees, who paid high prices for the land, could not meet their obligations, a fact which also affected the store owners who supplied raw materials and consumer goods, as well as the money advanced to the lessees to pay for the cost of harvesting. This conflict paralyzed activities during two months, seriously affecting exports.

In a political rally which filled Jacques with hope, Ezequiel Ramos Mexía, president Sáenz Peña's minister for Public Works and staunch defender of Patagonia and its enormous economic potential, allocated twenty million pesos (twenty per cent of the national budget) to the Promotion of the South, with the intention of extending railways from east to west, supplying the inhabitants of Patagonia with drinking water, dredging rivers, building irrigation dams and ports. This Promotion law involved an authentic agrarian policy and opposed the existence of large fiscal estates, favoring partition and sale of land belonging to the State. All this progressed well while Ramos Mexía was minister. But his plan collided with private interests, such as those of the British-owned Southern Railway, which looked suspiciously at the construction of railroads by the State that could become competitors. The minister had to weather a campaign of allegations and parliamentary impeachment, until he resigned in July 1913.

When Victorino de la Plaza became president, in August 1914, the activity of pioneers came to an end. The renowned geologist Bayley Willys, who had performed important work for Ramos Mexía, said about the parliamentary impeachment: "It illustrates the conflict between what was, what is, and what must not be: between Ramos Mexía, representing the intelligent governing class, the politicians

167

elected by the non-intelligent masses, and the Invisible Empire of capital, extending its control over both."

The Régime which had managed the country since the fall of Rosas in 1852 was showing cracks, and the political forces that composed it did not find the way to form a party to represent them. Jacques would later express his belief that one of the causes of the recurring crises that kept sapping Argentina's hopes, was the impossibility of the right to unite in one party to defend its interests and ideas. This impossibility would be on many occasions at the root of saber-rattling and military coups which prevented democratic life.

Jacques and André de Larminat had to return to France for their military service, which due to increasing belligerence had been extended to three years.

To make the trip to Buenos Aires, tired of bad roads and difficult accesses, the brothers decided to try the rivers. Taking advantage of a big tide on the Chimehuin they got into a boat, with bread, cooked chicken and a barrel of *chicha*. Rains had been so intense in that May of 1913 that on the first day the boat went speedily along, without the need of oars.

They camped on an island, and during the night the tide rose so high it lifted the boat to the top of some bushes, where it remained. When the tide subsided, they had difficulty in getting it to float again. Close to the crossing of the raft of Collón Cura, the shore to shore cable was hitting the water dangerously. They avoided it by taking the narrow branches of the southern coast, their rowing hampered by clumps of rushes.

Trying to sail down the river they met all kinds of trouble. Once the tide carried them in such a way that they shot like arrows through a grove of willow trees, skimming the water's surface. Obstacles were constant; on the west margin of the Limay they ran aground in a funnel of mud; in Piedra del Aguila they had to cross an extremely difficult sandbank with rocks; at Picún Leufú the river split in many branches, and the strong west wind pushed them to the shores time and again. When progress became quick due to the tide, they feared for their lives. No doubt they had embarked upon a perilous adventure, and at a certain point they thought that a miracle would be needed to prevent the boat from capsizing and being destroyed. The Limay river did not cease its surprises. Going through an area known as *Portal de los Rápidos*, the Rapids Gate, a number of eddies made the boat rotate and curve in all directions; in the Traful Grand Rapid the boat ran close to being smashed against a great rock, and following this the tide made them advance at top speed until they were deposited in shallow water, where they ran aground.

Tired of so many hazards, the brothers decided to proceed by land. They sold the boat, with the remains of the *chicha*, and hiked along the tracks of the railway under construction between Neuquén and Zapala, with the hope of finding the engine that returned to Neuquén. They did not find it, and had to complete the journey to the capital in a gig, with temperatures at eight degrees Celsius below zero.

The end of the tracks in Zapala would be laid only a month later, in July, and the first train would arrive the following year. By then, the assassination of Archduke Francis Ferdinand and his wife, in Sarajevo, would have triggered the Great War, one of the bloodiest in history, with the Larminat brothers serving in it.

Jacques went on business to different places in Buenos Aires, and then boarded ship for France with André. Upon arrival in his country for his military service, he joined an army cavalry unit. The atmosphere was heavy with movements of troops and the ominous bustle which preceded the outbreak of the Great War.

The world was going to war as "somebody who dives into the unknown". Argentina declared itself neutral. International disorder had run out control, and in 1914 the leaders of the great nations proved they lacked a clear idea of the consequences their decisions would generate. The war, expected to be short, lasted four years, and more than eight million men lost their lives.

Etienne, the brother who had remained at Cerro de los Pinos, received a telegram from a French friend, Combemale, giving him the news: "The war is on". The brief answer, typical of Etienne's personality, was: "Between who?". A few months later Etienne was also in France, enlisted as were his brothers.

Many people were surprised by the outbreak of war, in spite of the news that had been threatening conflict for some time. The Argentine banking system was unprepared. The belligerent powers had issued secret orders to their banks overseas to withdraw as much gold as possible from the countries that took no precautions against that eventuality.

From one day to the next astounded Argentines were left with only paper money, without the precious gold that they had hoarded during the bonanza years. Default amounted to twenty eight million in hard cash. The Argentine currency was immediately depreciated by ten per cent, and there was an overall rise in prices. President Victorino de la Plaza prohibited the exchange of banknotes for gold, and decreed a bank holiday. This affected the Larminats severely, because the French Bank of the River Plate retained their deposits until the end of the war, and only returned a minimum portion.

Although Argentina had declared itself neutral, a position that the government found hard to maintain –given the passions that the war sparked in the population, formed by a majority of European immigrants– the country defended its right to supply raw materials to all countries in the world, be they belligerent or not. This right was vital for a weak economy, which lived exclusively on such exchanges.

Jacques was posted to the 22nd Dragoons Regiment in Reims, the gallant cavalry force created by Napoleon in 1803. This regiment was famous for the prowess shown at Austerlitz, Iena, Moscow and Solferino, and in the Great War would renew its laurels at Le Havre, Yser and Saint Michel.

The uniform was a magnificent cuirass with a nickel coating and a helmet of the same metal with a crest of red horsehair.

Dragoons Regiment

Jacques left a vivid account of his experience in his War Diary, written with pungency and not without humor; it is a narration based on notes taken daily and drafted years later, interspersed with very good watercolors. Faith made him an inveterate optimist, and this gave way to heroism.

At the beginning Jacques was ordered to tasks so unheroic as the cleaning of stables and performing as the classic *cabot patate* (potato peeler), but as the war came nearer he was trained in the use of cavalry and charges. These started slowly, trotting, the gallop being reserved for the last meters. This procedure was necessary to maintain a straight line, so that the final clash would be more efficient. Charges were repeated between ten and fifteen times, in a long movement of flux and reflux, requiring an expert handling of horses.

171

At first, as from eight hundred meters, the firing of bullets from the artillery had to be endured; then, from four hundred meters on, grapeshot, and further on, artillery fusillade. All this was to be done dodging the fallen comrades, until the final assault against a wall of bayonets. If neither they nor their horses fell, and if they were not able to pierce the front or remained isolated, they had to try to pull back to the flanks, to rearm the squadrons and repeat the charge. French cavalry had enjoyed a great reputation in history.

One century before, Wellington had declared after Waterloo: "Gentlemen, do you by any chance ignore which is the best cavalry in Europe? It is the French cavalry. After personally suffering the effects of their daring and determination, I state that there is no other to surpass it."

And Stendhal: "Personal courage, firm temper, do not allow for hypocrisy. How can a man be a hypocrite when plunging against a wall of armed men?" It was not by chance that my grandfather belonged to this force. However, as will be seen, cavalry had become obsolete by 1914. At the end of the war, the numerous citations obtained for his conduct earned him the Legion of Honor, the War Cross and the Military Medal.

Jacques' War Diary begins thus: "At the end of July mobilization maneuvers were announced, and the war commission was appointed, but war seemed improbable, even impossible.

"Departure took place amid the cheering of the people. Long live the dragoons! Down with the Germans! The horses, coming out after a long rest, were scared by the shouting and the flashes the metals reflected, and they drew sparks from the pavement as they stamped their hooves. We set off full of confidence, with a feeling that we were following a planned order. If the platoon non-commissioned officer Mesdagh was a sad guy, a drunkard with doubtful manners, from whom the soldiers who were well-off bought favors, lieutenant de Marin, calm and collected, was loved by all. With a voice stirred by emotion he promised the platoon an unforgettable banquet if they passed near his castle in Lorraine.

Captain Wallace, his legs crooked after an accident he had with a horse, was a remarkable man for the exactness of his readiness and his sense of observation. His men were very proud of him. He believed much more in the effectiveness of a quick and precise shot than in sabers and swords, and communicated his point of view to his troops. And so it was that one day, when the regiment practiced target shooting, the squadron secured a fantastic result. "We later realized that one of us, driven by zeal, had multiplied the holes on the target, piercing it with a pencil". The squadron retained for a long time the name of "the squadron of the bullet hole". As for the colonel, he was Robillot, so admired and loved by his troops that they would have followed him right into hell.

"Painful marches were started towards Belgium, which Germany had invaded ignoring its neutrality. The stages were tough, and we rode up to seventy five kilometers at walking pace.

"Reception was enthusiastic everywhere, the people crowded to greet the troops as they marched through: bottles of wine, sweets, cakes, medals and scapularies that the men valued as much as the provisions. In some places donations of all sorts were so abundant that we had to get organized to receive them. In each line of four, the two outside horsemen dismounted and took the goods the people gave us, passing them to the two collector dragoons in the middle, who put them away in bags and haversacks.

"Marches became longer each time, and we only stopped for a few hours. The men wanted to sleep; eating worried them little. Feeling that the enemy was near, it was necessary to be more careful, but the men, exhausted, were dying to get some sleep. The more the advance progressed the more the need to sleep was felt, invading all of the troops. Nocturnal marches were a succession of stampedes and halts; the men were drowsy, and on opening their eyes and seeing nobody in front of them they shot off at a gallop, dragging the other laggards behind them. Fifty meters ahead they caught up with the top of the column, at a halt, and those following piled up and the lines twisted, breaking the formation, to restart the gallop shortly after. At each stop, no matter how short it was, the men dropped, to lie on the ground even if it was for just a moment... and mounted again, leaving behind their lances, which were lost in great number. Some of them did not wake up and remained there on a heap of stones, while their horses continued marching."

From those days Jacques recalled a demolishing fatigue, and little more: days and stages became mixed in his mind. He remembered that in the Luchy wood, the platoon arrived at eight p.m. at a big farm where a fine-mannered administrator, who could have passed for the owner, lived with his daughter. Jacques asked him where he could get something to eat for his men. –Dinner is not yet ready– was the answer –we will tell you when it is served– Half an hour later the man bade the platoon enter the dining room, where around a table sumptuously set, with a white tablecloth, silverware and flowers, thirty one-places had been prepared. The host invited the lieutenant to sit in front of him, with his daughter on the lieutenant's right and an NCO on his left, while the Dragoons, in awe, took their places around the table.

In Flavion, on August 15, the Dragoons met with the 3rd. Sappers Brigade, and Jacques was able to embrace his brother André, who had been assigned to that regiment. He would not see him again, for André fell in combat shortly after, in March 1915. He was twenty-two, and died from bullet wounds. The report that accompanied his post-mortem decoration said: "André de Larminat, non-commissioned officer, whose bravery and will inspired the admiration of all. Having returned voluntarily to the front after a first injury, he was mortally struck by several bullets, when at the head of his squadron he led a charge against the enemy trenches at Beauséjour."

Jacques was beginning to show his prominence. At Saint Martin there was a first engagement with Germans who were collecting fresh supplies, and Jacques led an offensive which forced them to abandon the truck loaded with goods, after setting fire to it. Captain

Wallace congratulated him and promised a report praising his action, for a decoration. But there was no time for that, because they were forced to withdraw hastily. Serious action began in Cambloux. The French were inferior in numbers, before a large concentration of German artillery. Greatly disappointed the combatants were ordered to retreat. At that stage, which would only end in Meaux, exhaustion was extreme and provisions were next to nil. The numerous war corps that had passed before had seen that no edibles were left in the area.

"Fortunately there are apples and beetroot that we can chew to alleviate hunger. The men become automatons and up to eighty kilometers are retreated each day, on extenuated horses dying of thirst. Many of these have their backs bleeding, because up to four days elapse before they are unsaddled. Some smell of infection, and it is necessary to draw them away to unsaddle them, because their wounds are nauseating.

"News is incoherent and contradictory. The advance of the Germans seems to be ruled by clockwork. In the morning, shells from the caliber 77 howitzers begin to fall; then, towards midday, heavy charges; in the afternoon, direct contact, and there is a cannonade of fire before they fall back at night. Our artillery works hard. We never sleep, the troops are shaggy, only half of them mounted, on deformed horses, dressed like nothing, but order and morale are perfect. Many are seen lagging behind, with whom there is indulgence if they steal to eat or dress, but there is no pity if they get drunk."

Jacques had proof of the latter when, on an occasion when he was aiding two abandoned comrades to help them eat with his platoon, he saw a general at the door of a bistro coldly shooting with his revolver those who left the place drunk.

"When they fight, the English fight well. But when teatime arrives, or night falls, the war is over for them. They break their formation without telling their neighbors, and they clumsily allow for surprise."

One day the regiment met an English cavalry brigade that was taking a bath in the river Oise with great noise, while their horses, fat and shining, were resting unsaddled. These Englishmen had given exhaustion as an excuse for their withdrawal, but it was not so. They were so well provided that they sold good knives for a few francs, and gave away buttons from their uniforms as souvenirs. When the English withdrew, the famished French found that hidden behind a haystack there were cans of corned beef and hams which had been abandoned.

The enemy's position was never known for certain, and upon spotting them, identification was not easy. The division in which Jacques fought was surrounded by British and Algerian troops who wore uniforms with unattractive colors, apart from being full of dust and bleached by the sun, which made them look similar to the Germans. Jacques, on the other hand was still wearing the colorful uniform of the Dragoons, which made an easy target for the enemy.

On September 1 the battle of Verberie was fought. The artillery division, backed by the cavalry, attacked the enemy during all of that day. The Belle battery lost four guns. In the afternoon the squadron retreated under drumfire, taking their wounded.

Jacques noted: "We have gone back even further. Reading the signs: 'Paris 62 kilometers', 'Paris 50 kilometers', 'Paris 45 kilometers' produces sad reflection. We are restless, but without losing hope. We are worried at seeing the troops disbanded, without a chief, bent on looting."

Near Chauconin they crossed fields covered with Moroccan marksmen. In no other place did he see so many corpses, lined up along the railway tracks. They all had their rifles broken in two: they had been trained to destroy their weapons before dying, to prevent the enemy from using them!

With his acid sense of humor, Jacques transcribes a dialogue that illustrates the condition of the cavalry.

"I bet you don't know what headquarters has just asked," De Neuville says to me. "What is the state of the horses that can still march."

"Really?"

"Yes, man. The captain answered that there are three that could trot for another three days: Emerald, Gayac and Dedeo. The others can only walk short distances."

"I think you're exaggerating slightly. Those horses need at least fifteen days to be able to stand."

And he adds: "Exhaustion is at the limit, men are all skin and bones, rations are sometimes missing, and we eat beetroot. Disgracefully, soldiers and even officers are in tatters, showing elbows and knees. But what remains most in our memories is the interminable hordes from the north, fleeing from the invader.

"Routes and fields are obstructed, people stunned and overwhelmed by misfortune, loaded with children and carrying their belongings in enormous bundles, processions of baby carriages, lots of old people, all of them famished, with sullen countenances, escaping forward without looking back.

"Women suckle their babies in the fields, there is not enough milk for the children, one must bump people aside on the roads to be able to get through. In Estoires, the bakers declared that on one single day one hundred and ninety thousand persons went to ask for bread. How did they manage to count them?"

In October, during the fighting in Vieille Chapelle and La Couture, Jacques was hit and fell; he tried to get up, but felt his leg was loose and heavy. His comrades helped him to reach the rear. He had been hit by three bullets, one of which had pierced his thigh and was lodged in his calf.

An ambulance transported him to the hospital at Béthune, but as they reached the paved road, with the excuse of an urgent call, they lowered him and left him in the street. He did the last stretch in a cart carrying beetroots, which would weigh heavily in his memory. At the hospital he was washed and cured by the nuns, who also gave him a bed and real sheets. About 10 that evening Jacques fell sound asleep, and at 4 p.m. on the following day they had to shake him to wake him.

"What? What's the matter?" he asked, still drowsy.

"Do you want to leave? There's a train..."

"A train? Right. Well, you know... in fact I'm in no great hurry. I would rather get some more sleep."

"But they've begun to bomb Béthune. Who knows if there'll be any trains after this one."

"Hell!" shouted Jacques, waking all of a sudden. "In that case there can be no doubt."

The journey was long and painful, seventy-two hours inside freight cars, only to progress a short stretch. At one of the stops a team of doctors went by, leaving Jacques looking ridiculous with an enormous red sign reading: "Apply anti-tetanus serum urgently". But they put him on board again without it, because there was none left.

In the suburbs of Paris the tracks were in a bad state, and the jerks of the wagons produced atrocious pain among the wounded. At last, on October 15, Jacques arrived at the 19th Complementary Hospital, sumptuously installed at the Régine Hotel. He was the first wounded soldier to be carried inside on a stretcher, while the nurses fluttered busily about him.

The wounds healed, but the bullet continued to be lodged in his calf. Jacques wanted to go to Blois to be operated on, and then complete his convalescence in the Annex I, which was none other than La Hardonnière, but there were strict rules about switching wounded military personnel from one region to another, and above all to send them to their families. In the end his obstinacy won the day, with the help of the doctors, and notwithstanding a large swelling, he made a long pilgrimage to Blois, where he was operated on twice. Finally on December 23, still with a noticeable limp, he departed for La Hardonnière, where he was able to celebrate Christmas with his family, and where he spent six excellent weeks recovering.

The year that was about to begin inaugurated the most memorable characteristic of this war: the trenches, with their stagnation. Those who had believed that this would be a short conflict had to admit their error. The initial enthusiasm had abated, giving way to reluctance, to rebellion, to desertion, and to widespread distress.

It was during that year 1915 that Italy declared war on Austria, Hungary and Germany, which meant a new front opened on the Alps. The fighting fronts were stabilized and there was no progress on either side. It was the "drôle de guerre", the strange war...

"When I returned to the front, in February 1915", Jacques wrote, "the war had changed substantially; now it was in the trenches. We would mount guard for four years running. Luckily we didn't know it, and we always hoped that come spring we would penetrate the wall and plunge through the opening in an irresistible charge.

"We lived expecting that moment, 'the hour of the cavalry'. Five times a month we thought the moment had come; five times each one of us was expectant, believing we were on the brink of battle, ready to launch ourselves... and five times, sad and disappointed, we had to turn back with our horses. In spite of the violence of the clashes, the wall did not budge."

Anxious to see the famous trenches, Jacques refused the possibility of being promoted to sergeant and thereby remain with the regiment stationed in the rear. He departed at the beginning of March as a non-commissioned officer for the trenches. (Bernard and Robert, the latter younger than Jacques, had joined as volunteers, also in the cavalry. They went through the war with their brother. They were called 'the Patagons').

"Our section was in Rivière, a few kilometers south of Arras. The helmet, without the horsehair crest, made our heads look quite round, with a very funny effect. Infantrymen, badly protected with their kepis, envied us. Entering the trenches was like walking into the night. They were no more than tombs. We footslogged our way across a sticky mud interminably, between two cold and viscous walls, through a maze of narrow passages that crossed in all directions. Badly coordinated trenches, without any signs, in which we invariably got lost, finally arrived head-on against a heap of branches where we got stuck, with the pressure of the column behind us. I remember the little second lieutenant, a newly-arrived novice, glued in the mud with no way out, furious and demoralized, who got a very bad reception when he arrived at about ten in the morning, to relieve those who had been waiting for him since midnight."

"As refuge for ourselves we had individual niches dug in the talus, where the whole of our bodies barely fitted. Seated with our noses against the yellowish, sticky wall of clay, we had all the time in the world to measure our disappointment... Not a single rifle shot! Long live spring and war on horseback! When we risked a look over the parapet to breathe some fresh air, all we saw was the immense plain, sad and naked, where, or so they told us, the Germans were entrenched just as we were, eight hundred meters away. We had to stay a long while silhouetted against the sky to hear a single shot, which invited us to return underground."

"War seemed to us long and monotonous; at headquarters they realized this, and tried to boost our morale by different means. One day Bernard and I, walking in a village, came across captain Pérez, of the High Command, who said to us: "I have just read in the *Echo* of Paris that a Larminat has died of his wounds. Is he a close relative of yours?" My brother and I looked at each other in anguish. We knew that André had been taken wounded to Paris, but our father had written saying that he was improving. A new letter confirmed this great loss."

"The cavalry advanced and retreated, and there were announcements of strong attacks which dissolved into nothing. The only real news was the constant transfers to which we were subject. The best chiefs were gone, apathy was rampant, and the cavalry, with its reputation as the best in France and in Europe, was being dismantled in stages, in favor of infantry. "Then, to diminish the easy visibility

of white horses, we were ordered to spread potassium permanganate over their bodies. After the first gallop sweat marked with
greenish channels the already unattractive hair; the visual effect was
repulsive."

"Quartered in the Bouvigny woods, some volunteers taught us
how to use grenades, which were then a novelty. I drew consolation
from not having tried, because those who did were most disappointed. They told how a dog would run barking after a grenade tossed in
the air, and watch it explode under its nose without being hurt.
Somebody said: "This thing is only dangerous for the user". And it
must be admitted that they were primitive. The Germans had begun
to use gas; we were given some small sacks with filthy gray fiber balls
soaked in hyposulfide as protection. In case of an alert, we had to
press them with our teeth".

"When we entered the Bouvigny wood we saw the soil turned
over by the recent attacks; pits among skimpy trees, dead bodies
everywhere, torn from their graves by the howitzer fire, or still
awaiting burial. We went to the end of the Éperon along extremely
narrow passages which progressed in zigzag, three or four meters
deep. We had to be quick, because the Germans were firing constantly. We finally got to about sixty or eighty meters from the
enemy, inside a trench that was interrupted by a wall. On the other
side it was German. Grenadiers from each army were separated only
by a few sacks of earth".

"We spent two days in absolute silence, without provisions or
water, behind our sacks of earth, in a perpetual night. We could not
even stand on the wall, because that was where German rifles, resting on trestles, aimed at us. A man got shot in the head that way, and
we had to bury him at the back of the trench, because every other
communication with the exterior was banned, except for the relief
and the evacuation of the wounded. Not without difficulty I got
permission to send for a can of water for my section; thirst was terrible in those summer days. The soldier who was sent was unlucky

enough to come across a second lieutenant who calmly drank three-quarters of the can."

"We tripped against hands and feet from the corpses, which emerged all over the place. If we dug the earth, the shovel would unveil worm-ridden bodies with a putrid smell. We were thirsty and sleepy. Only a few sacks of earth separated us from the Germans, who remained flat on the ground in a refuge camouflaged with leaves, so near to us that we imagined we could fight it out in a duel of grenades. Rifle shots were incessant right and left, although not against us; the artillery kept continuous action. Gunshots of every caliber, sounds and uproar, and at night we witnessed the incredible fireworks of the cannons."

During the battle of Champagne, well into the fall, the Dragoons thought the hour of the cavalry had finally arrived. After the confinement to the trenches, Jacques felt the pleasure of galloping amid the golden poplars, but when the attack on the Guillaume wood began, the intense artillery fire of the Germans made leaving the trenches an impossibility. In an attempt to advance, the French suffered enormous losses under machine-gun fire. In the end the Dragoons were evacuated to the north, to the area of Posnes. Jacques noted with bitterness; "Cavalry is dead for ever."

As a matter of fact, cavalry had become an anachronism. War was then fought mostly between airplanes, small black triangles in the sky followed by the white trails of bullets. In the front, the Germans found the winds were favorable for hurling their gases, and they did not refrain from doing so. All anti-gas material came into view: bottles of hyposulphite, alarm whistles, Vermorel sprays and instruction posters. "The clouds of gas passed to our right, because the German trenches were too close to ours. In those days we again enjoyed the marvelous fireworks of the alarm rifles."

In the harsh winter of 1916 the Germans opted for a war of attrition, and launched a tremendous offensive against Verdun, key to French defense under Pétain's command. During several weeks that area was an inferno that, even if it failed to break the front, left eight hundred thousand men dead. June saw the beginning of the battle of the Somme, which lasted five months and took the lives of a million soldiers. Such was the price of those two battles, military feats and human tragedies. The French had repelled the enemy and recovered almost every position they held at the beginning of the war. The enormous losses suffered by the Germans forced them to replace expert combatants with juvenile recruits.

Just like an octopus with tentacles, the lines and the trenches, two and three meters deep, multiplied; there were the first, the second and the third lines, plus the supporting and the reserve lines. In one word: in the fighting front, a strip of twenty kilometers was devastated.

"I received orders to remain for forty-five days in the area of La Source, three kilometers from the front, to update all the plans and maps that might be necessary. Apart from this, I had to deal with all communications and reports. I spent half my day measuring the trenches, making notes of mistakes, setting carrier pigeons free, sending mail and optic signals, and the other half day tracing beautiful colored maps, which fascinated my colonel.

"The area was immense, and the sun came down hard. As I had my feet in the shade and my head in the sun, and also before my eyes a brilliant white wall marked with black stones, which went up in vines and poppies, I developed quite an obnoxious summer ophthalmia. After having produced seventy-two colorful maps and walked a fantastic number of kilometers two and a half meters underground, I learned that my brothers were about to go on leave, and I obtained, with some difficulties posed by my colonel, permission to join them."

"Once we were back, days and months passed without anything to change monotony in that tranquil area. We passed from white mud to black mud; from the blinding gypsum-walled trenches to the clouds of dust of the routes of Tours-sur-Marne; we asked ourselves in terror if this deplorable life would ever end. It was no longer war, we fought nobody and we only mounted guard in front of the desert.

"Luckily, soon after we returned to the trenches in the Parroy wood, at the head of about fifty men, including Bernard and Robert. The war was not visible, except for in a few corners which, instead of being dug into the ground, were above it, and beside the trenches surrounded by earth walls. Lines had not yet been set, and we knew that our patrols crossed the German front line, and vice-versa. Where was the enemy? Before us we had a low and marshy plain, which descended to a small stream, the Sanon, where the Germans surely were. Every afternoon one of us, accompanied by two men, set off to cross the fences, keeping as low as possible. The plain was very damp; we slid in the mud, on the grass, always on the alert and ready at each step to come across the Germans. On those occasions we recalled the stories that were told about ferocious and silent dogs that accompanied the enemy patrols, and of the grenades that would explode in our faces if we touched the wires that held them. More than a war, it was a hunt."

"One evening Bernard and I left with three volunteers, Kerling, Provost and corporal Moulin. The weather was terrible. It was such a dark night that it was impossible to see anything a meter away; every now and then lightning lit the sky. We crossed the Sanon river and together with Kerling I posted myself against the right pillar of the bridge. Bernard went to the other side to stand behind the left pillar, while Provost and Moulin flattened themselves against the talus of the road. Hours passed in silence. Little by little our attention was weakened. Provost had to awaken Moulin three times, and I also felt my eyelids falling. I was considering crossing over to the other side to talk with Bernard to rouse myself, when suddenly I saw a silhouette stealthily bordering the right side of the bridge. I advanced one pace and had no doubt: it was a German patrol. He passed by me, half a meter away, without seeing me.

"But then another one followed, and then five or six more, all on tiptoes. The eighth man must have seen me, I could swear; surely a reflection on my glasses. So he threw at me a bayonet blow with his

At the end of a battle

rifle! I was expecting it, and so took him by his left hand, at the same time unloading my revolver in his belly. Did I kill him? In any case, the German fell with a great noise, dropping his rifle. That was the sign for battle.

"Bernard, for his part, lying in ambush like a dog on the bridge, had seen them coming, nine big silent bundles. Lightning allowed him to see their red raincoats; they were Bavarians, some armed with rifles and bayonets, others with revolvers, no doubt shod with soft footwear. He allowed them to advance, waiting for my signal; on my part, I had doubts whether to attack a troop of which I ignored its importance. The instinct of defense precipitated events; with a shot from his revolver Bernard knocked down one that was bending over the stone pillar. Bernard felt a blow on his left arm, from what he thought was a bullet. The German who had fired threw himself on Bernard, but Provost jumped on him from behind and after wrestling briefly he plunged his knife into the German's back. Provost, a sim-

185

ple man, never had faith in his revolver. Meanwhile (everything was happening at the same time, and the whole combat did not last more than seconds) Kerling, a Breton, calmly fired the six bullets in his revolver and saw at least two Germans fall to the ground. As for Moulin, he was assailed by an enormous German who encircled his whole body with a single arm; they rolled down the talus, but fortunately Moulin remained on top and blew his head off with a shot.

"Not a word was exchanged, merely about twenty shots. Fearing the proximity of the German lines, I ordered a retreat. We left at least six fallen enemies.

"Bernard, who was bleeding profusely, assured me that he could walk, but he was in a hurry to get back, and trembling from weakness. I was the last in the line, worried about Provost, who was missing. I left Bernard in Robert's hands and went back to the site of the combat with two new volunteers to look for my man.

"Clouds had gone, the night was less dark. We advanced sliding on the mud on one side of the road, under the talus; in that way we could see the silhouettes of the trees alongside the road. On top of the talus, three crouched silhouettes, like apple trees, were balancing strangely... Suddenly one of them stood up and moved a thin object that seemed a rifle...

"I jumped forward shouting 'Retreat!' and ran like a hare. The bridge was under observation and there was nothing to do. Fortunately, Provost had returned by the side of the wood. During the fight he had gone round so many times that he lost his bearings, and that was the reason he took longer to get back."

"Next morning colonel Secrettand came to congratulate us, and the story sounded high and loud in the Division. Bernard, who had received a deep bayonet blow, spent three weeks at the hospital of Saint-Nicolas-du Port and left for La Hardonnière for an eight-day convalescence. When he got back, colonel Secrettand decorated us three brothers, each one with the Croix de Guerre."

At the end of October a possibility appeared to join the "assault artillery", that is to say the tanks, and Jacques was quick to enter his name, ever anxious to try new experiences. It was not easy because there were many applicants, but by dint of insistence he got his way. However, before he joined the tank corps there was an episode he tells in his Diary, as was his habit, in an ironic vein.

"In November I was called to the regiment offices. I was already picturing myself inside a tank, but it was only a matter of going to Nancy by truck to receive from His Royal Highness the Prince of Connaught the 'British Military Medal', which I was awarded, it seems, for having been wounded with some Englishmen in a battle at Vieille-Chapelle. The ceremony was ludicrous. I was taught the lesson: one was supposed to say 'Thank you, sir', or 'I thank Your Royal Highness'. The Prince, who walked with a limp, had also tried to learn his phrases in French. When my turn came, he said:

'Ah! *Je suis très content de...* (I am very happy to...)

'*Merci, Monseigneur.* (Thank you, sir.)

'Ah! You! I say: *Je suis fort heurese de...* (I am extremely happy to...)

'*Je remercie votre Altesse Royale.* (I thank Your Royal Highness.)

'Oh, damn it!

And he pinned an enormous medal on my chest, just under my epaulette.

Two days later Jacques was on his way to Rupt Fort, delighted with his new assignment. It was at the Somme that the first tanks had appeared, armored cars that crawled on two roller belts over cogged wheels and which could pass over fences, trenches and other obstacles. Tanks were of little importance at the Somme, but in the campaigns of the following year, 1917, their participation was decisive.

"At Rupt Fort there was a mixture of officers and NCOs of every force, all of them volunteers, who had come hoping to wage war with a new and astounding means.

"Courses were short and well organized. One day general Estienne arrived, the pontiff who knew all the mysteries of the Army, and addressed us.

Renault tank regiment

"Let's see you, my friend. You come from the infantry?

"Very well. Three wounds?

"Very well. How many times have you been under enemy fire?

"Seven times.

"Well, you might be useful. I'll count on you.

"At the end he tells us:

"You know, if you don't think you can make it, leave as soon as possible. I shall not take it as treason; I only want volunteers. But in a month's time, it will be too late to leave."

Finally the tanks arrived, sixteen Schneiders, and on March 7 they left for Champlieu. Getting the caterpillars to move over the frozen soil was a hard job.

"It was night; crossing the wood was like a poem. The 'zinzins'

188

(the tanks) that we did not know yet how to drive by day, by night we crashed into the trees, and arrived quite beaten at the barracks where we had been assigned."

"We formed part of a long chain of the Hadrian barracks, which occupied a semicircle of two leagues at the border of the wood. There were nine groups already. Every day new ones arrived, and it was the most incredible reunion that can be imagined, since the officers kept their own uniforms, and there was a pick of everything: flyers, seamen, gunners, sappers, French and Algerian infantry, dragoons, marksmen, chasseurs on foot, on horseback, from Africa, from the Alps, even a black captain. All this led to merriment; invitations were sent from one group to the other, we played tennis, it was a real holiday."

"At a given moment drill began, carried out in the plain and in the wood; we had to follow such precise rules that it was obvious that they were nothing but theory. The Schneider tanks had three defects: vision was poor due to the narrow slot of the visors, and when the Germans learnt to shoot at these slots, they became altogether useless. Fans were badly placed; the heat inside rose to over fifty-five degrees Celsius, and at that temperature the air became saturated with fumes of gasoline. Lastly, the gas tanks, made with very thin plates, had been placed inside before the legs of the drivers, and would explode under the first shell, carrying the occupants to a horrendous death. This was solved by placing the tanks outside and at the back, in two armored trunks protected internally, with such good results that shells could run across the gas reserves without making them explode. The direction of the air intake of the fans was also modified. Visibility continued to be poor, and it was only little by little that they gave us periscopes. The armor was prominent for its thickness. Only some piercing bullets were able to perforate the steel, and extra plates were added in the front parts that were more exposed.

"Time went by slowly, while we maneuvered non-stop on the plain, strewn with an interminable web of trenches. We received all sorts of visits, sometimes entire regiments that ended doing maneuvers with us. All the line infantry came along, chasseurs on foot, Algerian, Senegalese. But the moment arrived when the gasoline consumed was so exorbitant, that the officers concocted the ridiculous idea of having us represent on foot the tanks in the fields, each one of us in his place, making the gestures each one would make inside the contraption! The only detail missing in this comedy was to have the gunners shout boom! for each imaginary explosion, and for the machine-gunners to rotate a wooden rattle.

"Another mania of the High Command was the 'Hébert calisthenics', which we had to perform at dawn, half naked: an appalling display of bald heads and middle aged bellies in grotesque positions. The slowness with which the material was delivered forced us to fill time with this drill, or with other pastimes: we looked after the orchard and the kitchen garden, we raised pigs, chickens, rabbits; we read the Navy Bulletin, played tennis and even organized tournaments. Every now and then shows were staged in the Roman theater; the acoustics of this big amphitheater with its grass tiers was excellent.

"To while away time, officers in the group placed a request for godmothers in the magazine *Parisian Life*. It was the fashion! In a few days one hundred and ten answers had arrived, in blue and in rose stationery, with initials, in every format, some of them including photographs, some sincere and moving, most of them pretentious, emanating aggressive perfumes.

Then some more began to roll in from overseas. Two from Algiers, one from the Antilles, one from Sudan, one from Madagascar. Each of us selected the ones he wanted to answer. My friend Renaudière chose no less than seven, devoting himself to an unrestrained correspondence, with the aim of choosing one. A month later he said to me: "I got it! I've found her, she's Violet. I have asked her for a date! Look at what this little angel writes to me". And he made me read a series of phrases, obscure and bombastic, to sum it all up thus: "This little thing must be charming". And he set off for Paris.

"He returned the next day, dragging his soul. He had been greeted at the station by an old lady, wealthy and withered, mutton dressed up as lamb, who threw herself into his arms rolling her eyes. It was Violet! "You'll think I fled. Well, no. To avoid giving a bad impression, I stood her a beer at a bar".

The year 1917 ended with momentous news. It was the Russian Revolution, by which the Bolshevics seized power. In the first months of 1918 the Germans launched a great offensive on French soil, and were able to penetrate sixty kilometers into the line of trenches. During the night airplanes bombed Compiègne and Paris. On March 21, raining fire from four thousand pieces of artillery a battle started which lasted seven months. The defeats of the British at Ypres and the French at Chemin des Dames allowed the German troops to advance to sixty-five kilometers outside Paris. But the desperate counterattack by the Allies in Compiègne stopped the offensive, and shortly after the United States entered battle, a decision which guaranteed the outcome of the war, Jacques wrote in his Diary about those days.

"The appalling 1914 parade on the roads was being re-enacted. For the second time, whole towns fled before the German advance. People had barely enough time to repair the damage, to again escape. They looked sullen and disheartened, wandering about exposed, hunched under their bundles and loaded with children. We picked up some who were exhausted.

"On June 11, 1918, we were ordered to attack Mery. In perfect order, each battery advanced with three tanks in line, one in the rear, and its infantry in reduced columns marching fifty meters behind. Not a gunshot, nor an airplane, nor a bullet. It was obvious that the enemy did not expect an attack, and surprise was complete."

Suddenly the French opened fire and continued advancing in the midst of gunshots and machine-gun fire, trying to gain territory before the reaction of the enemy, which did not take long. The shell from a mortar exploded on the right side of the tank that Jacques commanded, damaging the armor, ejecting the machine-gun turret and causing panic inside.

The mechanics for each group followed the tanks on foot at a short distance, entrusted with the necessary repairs. So a few minutes later the one assigned to them appeared. His name was Tyrel du Poix, a burly man with a neatly-trimmed beard who, while bullets whizzed past, began a difficult job, because the armor had been pushed in. Nevertheless, he went about his business with absolute calm, just as if he were repairing a car in an avenue in Paris.

"Suddenly we heard a shout: 'German counterattack!', while the infantry began to pour in from all sides in great disarray. I looked at Poix. Wielding a monkey wrench, he carried on with his job, unruffled. What was to be done in the midst of a retreat? I got into Renaudière's tank and found it full of people who had thought it wise to seek refuge there. I proceeded to evict them, and keeping the three assistants that were necessary, set off to catch the other tanks. But at that moment a machine-gun that was too close fired bullets at my glasses, breaking them, my cheeks and neck, plus one which pierced my nose on one side. Blinded by the blood, I told captain Lévèque: 'I have the impression that I am heading in the right direction, but I cannot see. Please direct me with your periscope' 'Right!' he answered, and immediately shouted: 'March forward, third speed!' I couldn't understand why, but I obeyed. I thought that maybe another counterattack was on. We carried on two or three hundred meters, until I heard him shout to me: 'Halt!' I got ready to shoot. But there was not a noise. I turned around. 'So? Nobody shoots? Where is the captain?' 'Oh, the captain went back to his refuge.' 'Where are we?' 'Beside your broken down tank. Oh, but you are badly wounded, my second lieutenant!' Quite right, I was covered in blood, which had even filled and overflowed my gas mask, hanging from my neck. Without glasses, I could not see a thing. Furious against Lévèque, I went to look for the admirable Poix, who was carrying on with his repair, impassive, under a hail of bullets and increasing explosions of shells. He greeted me angered."

"You made a disaster advancing suddenly, like a madman. I had almost finished, and you crashed the tank! Now, I don't know if I'll be able to do it all over again.

"Well, man, I'm really sorry. I felt a crash, but I didn't think it was important.

"Okay," said Poix, calming instantly, "you stopped dead when the Germans counterattacked. But you're bleeding like an ox, it looks serious.

"No, it's superficial. I'm going to change my glasses. Where is that pig Lévèque?"

"That's his refuge. He must be in there."

"As a matter of fact there he was, with the captain of the company that headed the attack troops."

The battle was bloody. US aviators, unable to distinguish French tanks from German tanks, shot unceasingly. In Jacques' narration the scenes of heroism alternate with tragedy. He witnessed the death of many of his comrades, and others fell prisoner, and the majority, like himself, were wounded. All in all, they were able to recover Mery. In the following month Jacques was decorated for this action.

The German troops and people were subjected to strict rationing, and the sudden improvement in the provisions of the Allies, guaranteed by the British navy, plus the entry of the United States into the war, demolished their morale. Against a seriously discouraged army, the Allies endeavored to start a series of offensive movements which put an end to the war in a few months.

Six hundred thousand men from the United States compensated for the losses suffered in the previous campaign, and hundreds of light tanks, of great mobility, constituted an incomparable instrument to disrupt the enemy defenses. The initiative remained in the hands of the Allies as from July 18, when Mangin carried out a surprise attack against the German bulge in the South with three hundred light tanks, taking thirty thousand prisoners. Jacques narrates the attacks of July 19 and 20, in which he participated:

"There was a hail of bullets, and the tank, badly articulated, with the turret crooked because of a blast, lets shrapnel in abnormally and one piece hits me in the right eye. Lombard, the young corporal gunner, shouted at me that they'd killed the machine gunner on the right, and that his assistant was wounded... They were firing at us from a small wood. Two more splinters penetrated my cheeks and my neck, this time on the left; the wound in the neck prevented me from turning my head. Lombard started moaning again; there were two more wounded, and so was he. I kept on going forward, and seeing that east of the wood there were nothing but Germans, I stopped and started shooting; the enemy fire had become unbearable and had to be stopped, while waiting for the other tanks. Lombard said that he could not shoot, and that there was nobody backing us. I advanced, and we remained as a very visible target in the middle of the plain. All machine-guns in front were firing at us. The hail of bullets was terrifying. Lombard, with a sepulchral voice, announced: "My second lieutenant, every single man is wounded". But seeing that I am not stopping, he said: "My second lieutenant, every single man is dead". I stopped and asked: "Well, let's see. Who's dead?" There was no answer. In spite of the rigidity of my neck, I managed to look back. The scene was appalling; the whole crew was lying in a sea of blood. Outside, bullets crackled unceasingly against the armor. Well, I did not want to drive a hearse into the German lines. My neck was swelling rapidly, so I resigned myself to withdraw".

This action earned Jacques his third decoration. In the month of August, the German defeats followed rapidly. At the end of September, with the assault on the Siegfried line, their resistance crumbled. There were still battles raging for another month, but Ludendorff had already communicated to the German government that it was necessary to call for peace. On October 5 the armistice was called, and it was signed on November 11, in a wagon in Marshal Foch's special train, in the Compiègne wood. The long nightmare had come to an end.

The Larminat family had suffered another loss in the last days of the war. André had fallen at the beginning of the conflict, and close to the end, in July 1918, Bernard died, aged twenty-four, struck by three machine-gun shots as he advanced at the head of his platoon in the Montvoisin offensive, south of the Marne.

Of the last battles Jacques kept a recollection of exhaustion, due to rheumatic fever and the poisonous gas he had inhaled. And in spite of feeling sick and nauseated, the possibility of remaining blind, with wounds, ulcers and even convulsions, with only a trace of a voice and with a frame of mind that he defined as disastrous, he gathered strength enough to receive the Legion of Honor from colonel Chadeville. The citation for which he was honored with this distinction was drafted as follows:

"French Army, Legion of Honor.

Jacques de Larminat was prominent in all the battles against the enemy in which he took part, especially in May 1917 and June and July 1918. During the battles of September 26, 27 and 28, 1918, he was assigned to secure, within a totally devastated area, the entrance of the armored vehicles into the combat line. Advancing with the assault waves, he managed with his inspiring courage and his indomitable energy to overcome considerable difficulties, defying the violent enemy fire, achieving in this way a personal participation in the success in those events. Signed, Commander in Chief, Marshal PÉTAIN."

The Organization
of the Family

Don Santiago and his young wife Magdelon arriving in Cerro de los Pinos, 1920

En noches serenas, soñando a mi lado
mareados de luna y ensueño los dos,
sus ojos miraban el cielo estrellado,
pensando en el puerto del último adiós.
Pasajera rubia de un viaje lejano
que un día embarcaste en un puerto gris
¿Por qué nos quisimos, cruzando el océano?[34]

HÉCTOR PEDRO BLOMBERG

HE FIRST OF THE BROTHERS TO BE DEMOBILIZED was Etienne and he decided to return immediately to Cerro de los Pinos with the Ligers, who had been in France since the beginning of the war. The brothers were anxious to know what had become of the *estancia* during those four years without news, and with German neighbors that could have been hostile.

The journey was interminable for Etienne, who recorded in his diary how much emotion he felt to be returning to those lands which were part of him. And although he admitted that Patagonia was gray, monotonous and at times uninteresting, as soon as he set foot in his home he recalled the green of the land in summer, the woods, the

---

[34] *"On serene nights, dreaming beside me*
"Both of us dizzy with moon and reveries
"Her eyes looked at the starry sky
"Musing on the port of the last farewell
"Blonde passenger of a distant journey
"That one day went on board in a gray port
"Why did we love each other crossing the ocean?

Héctor Pedro Blomberg

rivers and the mountains, the blue fog and the distant horizon, the shadows of clouds over the landscape full of sunlight. He felt that he was back home. The call of the wild birds made him smile again, and had the deep joy of seeing proof that the loyal and efficient Gallardo Lavalle had managed the *estancia* with a sure hand, and that in spite of all the problems Cerro de los Pinos remained as they had left it and was operating marvelously. (Years later, the family would obtain from the Foreign Relations Ministry of France a decoration for "French merit" for the foreman, with a tricolor ribbon, a diploma and a letter of acknowledgment from the president of the French Republic).

Jacques arrived at Cerro de los Pinos in September, three months after his brother. He had been delayed by matters of the heart: he was traveling after his engagement to his beloved Magdelon, Magdelon Doé de Maindreville, who had been his support and hope during the war years. They set the date for the ceremony: they would marry in France on February 26, 1920, and travel immediately to Argentina, where they would set up their home.

Bernard and André were no longer with them. As a result, it was decided that François and Robert would join in the Argentine enterprise. The former gave up his career as a seaman, married and took up residence on the *estancia*, with one child. Robert for his part abandoned his examinations at the École Polytechnique and traveled in November, to substitute for Jacques, who had to return to France to marry.

The wedding took place in Versailles, at the Saint Louis cathedral, with all the pomp and magnificence that postwar France could allow herself, and with many friends and relatives. Jacques and his bride enjoyed the first spring colors at La Hardonnière, and in the early days of April boarded ship for Argentina as a honeymoon trip, in the company of the Thierrys, two brothers who were friends of the newlyweds, and wanted to see the severe beauty of Patagonia. Their stay in Buenos Aires was brief; Jacques promised Magdelon that when their first offspring was born they would stay longer in the city, so that she could get to know it better. On April 22, 1920 the young couple took the train for the first time to Zapala, a line which had been inaugurated shortly after Jacques had left for France. They had a thirty-six hour journey, in a narrow and dirty car, with no room for the luggage.

Magdelon's first impression, once they left the green fields of the pampas, with the thick woods in the *estancias*, was that the landscape was too flat and quite ugly. She still had to see the desert-like aridity of Patagonia.

In Zapala an old Mercedes Benz car awaited. It was in a dilapidated state but had room for all, and broke down seventeen times before reaching the *estancia*. Magdelon had never seen so much dust, and laughed incredulously when the driver, who was all the time using his ability as a mechanic, asked them to get off so the car could reach a sandy crest with less weight. The first night stop was at Catan Lil, a *pulpería* half way between Zapala and Cerro de los Pinos, and it was there that Magdelon understood why Jacques had said so much about the Patagonian hardships and shortcomings. For the last lap of their picturesque journey, an ox-cart awaited them to cross the Chimehuin, where they were escorted by a cohort of farmhands, who paraded behind the newlyweds with shy curiosity. Etienne and Robert gave them a warm welcome, and Magdelon felt comforted upon hearing the Solognese accent of the Ligers, whose children Riri and Tita awaited with enormous bouquets of flowers gathered in the *estancia*.

Although for the bride it meant a radical change in her life, she proved equal to the occasion. And there were beauties which compensated for the discomforts. The "Old Estancia" was in the middle of a park with willows, apple trees and bushes like rosemary, *cedron* and lavender, which perfumed the air in spring. The house was tiny; it only had three rooms, distributed among the brothers; one of them was the dining room, with a big table in the middle. On the southern margin of the Chimehuin the house destined to Jacques, François and their families was under construction, but considering the carpenter's slow pace, moving into the "Southern Estancia" would take some time.

Jacques had a lot to do, but also much to show Magdelon, who was discovering the imposing landscapes around. They filled the last warm days of the fall roaming about the river and fishing big trout, hunting ducks and great bustards, all of which they ate heartily, alternating the monotonous diet of mutton.

The wind never ceased blowing, and a day that in France would have been very windy was considered balmy. Animals were used to it, but trees, bushes and flowers suffered, and even were uprooted by the strength of the wind. And dust and sand were a constant bother.

Magdelon, who showed the same passion as her husband for nature and spent much time outdoors, had to get used to being covered in dust, and hardly ever wash her arms above the elbow. There a line marked the limit of the reach of the water.

However, she was delighted to go out riding, as was Jacques. Their favorite excursion was to the summer fields, close to the Andes, where for leagues on end they bordered the wall of rock that changed colors with the sun. On clear mornings they were accompanied by flocks of ibises which mixed their gray and yellow plumage with the colors of the red, green and yellow beeches. The winter air, with its piercing cold, could already be felt.

The May rains forced the races and dances, which traditionally were part of the patriotic celebrations, to be held in the mud. And soon after, snow covered everything. Isolation and the overflowing of rivers were normal inconveniences, and that winter of 1920 was especially harsh. The tide of the Chimehuin rose above its historic record (one meter ninety), flocks were lost in the snow, work in the fields was hampered because the horses were soon exhausted, having to struggle against the meter-deep snow that covered the ground.

The period that elapsed between one inspection and the next produced ugly surprises, such as the flight of the best flock of Ram-

Inside the house

bouillet sheep. (Jacques, who always found a humorous formula to apply to misfortunes, announced that this incident had been caused by the "law of the unfinished fence") The Collón Cura river swept away the telegraph lines, leaving the house isolated and with no post for a month.

There were nights when the wind blew with such fury that it would shake window frames, doors and furniture; there were moments when they feared that the whole house would be blown away. Drafts of cold air burst in through the slits in the wooden structure, so that maintaining a reasonable temperature inside proved difficult. Working in the open was torture, with the wind lashing faces like a whip, leaving hands purple and numb. Sandstorms enveloped everything, and there was not enough protection to prevent the eyes from being constantly bloodshot.

And even so, that was not the harshest reality of Patagonia, as it became clear to Magdelon when she saw people who came to the *estancia* asking for shelter for a few nights, or for the basic foodstuffs. One evening a Chilean family with ten children in tatters asked permission to sleep in the barn; the children were unshod and dirty, dressed with burlap and obviously hungry. That kind of scene was repeatedly witnessed.

One consequence of destitution was robbery, the last resort of unemployment, and relatively easy to put into practice, given the great distances and isolation. The Larminats knew the problem well, and in spite of having the flocks and their shepherds well organized, each year's branding, baths and shearing, showed that it was a difficult evil to eradicate.

Winter also brought for the brothers a peculiar pleasure. It was the moment to begin planting, and Jacques was impatient to try the species he had brought from France. The Larminats' love for trees has been mentioned, coming from several generations, but in the case of my grandfather it was a passion, which he transferred to his descendants. The love he felt for trees was stronger than the wind, which many times wrenched his most precious specimens. On that first winter Jacques started a job which would continue throughout his life. He planted many trees (plum trees, maritime pine trees, araucarias, poplars, weeping willows, oaks), and kept doing so well into spring. Today there are more than one hundred different species in the park of the *estancia*. When we, his grandchildren, visited La Hardonnière, in the seventies, we found something in common with the woods at Cerro de los Pinos: the same order, the same rhythm and the same scents. Even the smells of the old castle brought memories of those at our grandfather's house. We understood how his nostalgia had given him the energy to rebuild his home on the other side of the world, with the same spirit.

Winter was also the period in which pigs were slaughtered to make hams and sausages and vary the diet of the *estancia*. The Ligers taught Magdelon how to smoke meat and how to make use of the last drop of blood, a task which did not particularly please the young lady, who by then, was pregnant.

Good weather brought back the visitors. The most peculiar character was a neighbor, Andrés von Puttkamer, the "Freiherr", as Jacques called him, a German noble exiled by his family to remote Patagonia. A descendant of the powerful Bismarck, it was said that a physical impairment determined his fate since he was born. He studied in the best schools in Europe, but as he became an adult his parents got in touch with the Argentine consul to find an adequate site where their offspring –who would receive part of his fortune in land– could be sent, a place that he would never leave. Patagonia, for its remoteness, was the ideal place. So in 1908 the young Puttkamer arrived, with enough capital to build on his land a big German-style palace, but also with sufficient spite to challenge all the rules of civilized life. His relationship with the Larminats was cordial, although with bursts of eccentricity inherent to his personality. During years they litigated politely to determine the exact place where the fence separating the *estancias* should run, where to plan the road to Zapala, or the crossing, always complicated, of the Collón Cura. During the war Gallardo Lavalle had to put up with all kinds of affronts from a hostile German neighborhood, who threatened to expropriate French land, and Puttkamer was the most hostile of them all. But, as years went by, the Larminats and Puttkamer developed a close friendship. In fairness, the German was a cultured and polite man; the parties he gave in his great castle were a real experience. Having been deprived of his rank, he did not care much for forms, and let himself be carried away by his fiery temper. He was fond of a good table, and his dinners flowed with wines which he made. He had a passion for motorcars, and every year he would surprise his neighbors with the latest models in automobiles, which fared badly on the appalling southern roads. He used to go armed, since his name as a millionaire had lured more than one bandit, and he ended up being feared even by outlaws.

One day the "Freiherr" invited my grandfather to a typical lamb barbecue, and before sitting at the table, prompted him to visit the large cellars in the house. At a given moment Puttkamer went into a garret and came out with a burlap sack. He extracted from it the helmet of a French soldier of the Great War with a bullet hole on one side, and showed it to my grandfather saying with a big smile: "Look, don Santiago, this is a memento I brought from the front, in my wartime; this is how we left our enemies. I'm very sorry for your compatriot!" As he could not stomach the effrontery, my grandfather answered, as if reluctantly: "Oh, that... look, when the war was over I had so many German helmets with a hole that I had to leave them behind, because of the weight. My sisters turned them into flowerpots for geraniums! What a pity, if I had known that you were interested in them, I would have brought them".

As was normal in those times of isolation, Puttkamer led a married life with a Mapuche woman who originally had gone to the *estancia* to clean and to cook. He had many children with her. They grew up like real gauchos, without keeping any connection with their German family and ignoring the meaning of the coat-of-arms, an enormous shield that presided over the majestic dining room of the castle.

Other neighbors were the Reids, who contributed their good English manners. A visit to the *Gente Grande estancia*, which Mr. Reid managed, meant a return to civilization. Jacques often accepted invitations for dinner, unpacking with pleasure his elegant dinner jacket and his white shirt, to be on a par with his hosts. Full-blooded sheep people, the Reids had the best animals in the region, although much later the Larminats managed to wrest from them the Australian Merino Grand Champion prize at the Rural Show in Palermo, Buenos Aires, a trophy that had always been in the hands of the two big English *estancias* of the zone, *Leleque* and *Maquinchao*.

But the most frequent visits were those that were unexpected, and generally by unknown people. The traditional Patagonian hospitality was an inviolable rule in those regions, and whoever the visitor was he would be offered food and lodging. Invariably they were received with pleasure, because routine was put aside and they were a good excuse for changing the topics of conversation. In the *estancia* diary which the Larminats kept innumerable visits have been recorded, by all manner of characters, who usually arrived in summer:

"On his way to *estancia Gente Grande*, where he is going in search of employment, Mr. Diamond, an Englishman, stopped. He is an amiable young man, who fought the war in the Dardanelles and Flanders; he was wounded, and had four brothers killed. Enlisted at sixteen and sent to the front, he is twenty-three and is looking for a way to make a living."

"At midday, we saw a whole cavalcade approaching: two ladies, a gentleman, a farmhand, all on horseback and followed by five horses carrying the luggage. They introduced themselves and explained. They are Henri Combemale, his wife and his sister-in-law, Miss Durand. They come from Chile to spend a few days here, and they had announced their visit by a mail which of course never arrived. They are not difficult to satisfy. The ladies are talkative and very polite, and make use of the visit to tune Magdelon's piano. They are versed on the subject and they play some pieces."

"An Armenian priest with a layman from the same country, sent four years ago by the patriarch of Vanqueter to aid their orphans, pass by. He has traveled throughout much of Argentina; we donate twenty pesos. He talks a lot about the war he fought on the Russian side, of the Turks whom they despised, so much so that they pretended to make them abjure their faith, or leave the country. He has a bayonet cut in a finger."

"A young doctor sent by the Ministry of Hygiene stays for the night, with a police officer, two policemen and some others. Smallpox has been declared at the MacDonald estate, and the police, armed to the teeth, are ready to fight it."

The irony of this last annotation is repeated in others, as in the account of the visit by a doctor, recently installed in Junín de los Andes and who was on the lookout for patients. In an appalling

The three brothers and Magdelon

French and assuring he loves to speak that tongue, the little doctor drinks large glasses of cider and devours everything that goes his way, after which he asks:

"Has doctor Vehrerbrüghen done good business here?"

"Yes," Jacques answers, very seriously. "Very good business. He ended up completely broke."

The doctor complains about Argentina's health, that leaves him with no patients.

"And do you know Dr. Schumann, of Mamuil Malal? Has he got patients there?"

"I understand," replies Jacques, "that down there only guanacos are found. Although perhaps Schumann has bought sheep to be able to cure them."

"And who cures the farmhands here?"

"They get cured on their own, and they never die."

The doctor tells them that he found the hotel at Junín de los Andes where he stopped to be very inferior, until he rented a room at the home of a man who is almost a hundred, to whom he metes out his treatments. Jacques answers:

"Poor man, he has lived one hundred years without medicines or illnesses, and before a year is over you will have killed him."

Health was a real issue in Patagonia, although it was considered a very healthy region, in spite of its harshness. But isolation imposed difficult tests, as in the case of sudden illness, accidents, wounds or childbirth. The enormous distances between *estancias* and towns, the rigors of weather and the little confidence inspired in the area by doctors who charged steep fees and were frequently mediocre practitioners with doubtful diplomas, gave *curanderas*, the women country healers, a solid reputation.

The country folk felt so much mistrust for doctors as gullibility before *curanderas*, who sometimes committed severe damage to the body of patients. Jacques mentions in the *estancia* diary many cases of "sage women" (midwives) who imposed their medicines, be they herbs on a woman with a tumor that had burst, or a poultice of fat and herbs, plus a precarious framework made with canes, to a farmhand with a broken leg.

On one occasion a *machi* from Malleo went to the *estancia*, a young witch who sang invocations followed by spasms to drive away the *gualicho*, the devil. Some *estancieros* had decided to tend their sick themselves, and there was one who made quite a name for himself on an *estancia* around Nahuel Huapi.

All considered, Jacques had promised Magdelon that when the birth of their first child approached, they would travel to Buenos Aires, to be seen by good professionals. At the end of spring the date was getting near, so in early December the couple left the *estancia* aboard a Citroen which after many breakdowns finally left them in Zapala, where they took the train.

They arrived in Buenos Aires and Jacques was able to be equal to his promise and show his wife the city, as far as the heat and her pregnancy would allow. Bernardo, the eldest, arrived in the world in the afternoon of December 25, 1920. Before returning they waited for the arrival of François, his wife and daughter, who came from France to join the family enterprise. They all went back by train, and once on the *estancia* the married couples set up their homes in the house built on the south shore of the Chimehuin, which from then on was known as the "Southern Estancia", to differentiate it from the "Old Estancia", where all of them had lived until then.

From that moment on, the Argentine lives of the Larminats followed an even rhythm, though not monotonous, of work, enterprise, children, joys and sorrows. My grandfather was already "Santiago", or don Santiago, and his brothers also used names turned into Spanish. Esteban, the only one who remained single, left for France with the intention of getting married, and Roberto remained in charge of the "Old Estancia".

The other house, where Santiago, Magdelon and the newborn installed themselves, with François –now Francisco– and his family, hardly provided the basic comforts. This house, built with wood from the area and with no more shelter than an old *chacay*, posed the challenge of its desolate air. Everything was waiting to be done: the park, the kitchen garden, the henhouse, the sheds, the house for the laborers, the chapel, the bath for the sheep, a warehouse for the apples... It was hard to imagine that sandy dale transformed into an *estancia* in operation. But that is what they had gone there for, and there was no time to waste.

Santiago took up the organization of the library, and Magdelon removed the dust from her beloved art deco style Pleyel piano, which had accompanied her from France and which she was so fond of playing. It must have sounded strange to hear the classic compositions rising against the brutal howling of the wind. But they were a relief from nostalgia, and a distraction during evenings.

These were as a rule calm, but shocks were not in short supply. For instance, at that time cattle or sheep drivers could be dangerous as they passed along the southern route, close to the *estancia*; if they found no security, they stole everything they could lay their hands on: provisions, horses, clothes on a clothesline, at the same time scaring the dwellers with their hoarse laughter and their shouts. They could be seen approaching wrapped in a cloud of dust, along the "route", a dirt road with a fence on both sides, which ran scarcely a hundred meters from the homestead. Sometimes the drovers took five thousand sheep, or hundreds of heifers, driven by five or six farmhands who had done a thousand kilometers and still had a long stretch to go before reaching Chile, where they could get good prices. When they passed by night, women trembled in their beds, while the men, armed, stood guard.

There were also alert calls of another nature, as some of the previous dwellers in the area, before the construction of the house, tried to get back to their old habitat, and this fauna had to be convinced that they should seek other horizons.

In the chronicles of the *estancia* Santiago left a funny rhyme illustrated with a watercolor, about a large armadillo that kept them in suspense for many nights with the sound of its hoofs scratching the wood, trying to get into the house.

Vers minuit on entend un vacarme effroyable
Madame, effarouchée, reveille son époux:
"Des rats ont pénétré, leur troupe est innombrable
Et ils vont dévorer les nez de nos chers choux"
"Ma Bonne, calme-toi. Ce bruit vient du dehors
Et je vais, sous vos yeux, mettre la horde en fuite."
"Fuera!" Crie-t-il d'abord, et le chien s'enfuit vite.
Mais le bruit continue...
Horreur! S'offre à sa vue
Un énorme tatou, puant, velu, très sale,
Qui s'efforce à violer la chambre conjugale!
Le Cogérant, très bravement,
A saisi la fauve aux aisselles

Et d'un grand geste large, à épater les belles,
Il envoi le hideux cloporte
A la porte...

It is midnight; a terrible noise is heard
The lady, scared, wakes her husband
"—Rats have come in, an immense troop
" They will eat our children's noses.
"—Take it easy, dear, the noise comes from outside
" You'll see how I put the horde to flight
Out! he shouts, and the dog escapes
But the sound goes on
Horror! before his very eyes
An extremely large armadillo, smelly, hairy, very dirty
Tries to break into the matrimonial chamber.
The man, with great courage
Takes the beast by the armpits
And with an imposing effort
Which would fascinate the beauties
Sends the horrible creature out
Through the door

In an orderly fashion each of the brothers kept a careful diary of all that happened on the property. My grandfather noted not only the work done, which was considerable, but also the weather and the pace of the scant social life of each day. Work was no different from that of other southern *estancieros*: how the flocks developed, the dates for harvesting potatoes, apples and wheat; the separation of sheep, the dips, the branding, the cures, the purchase of materials, the construction work, etc.

A characteristic of the Larminats was the pace they set for their work, but this did not prevent my grandfather from recording in amusing verse the events worth noting, and illustrating them with

Crossing the Chimehuín

watercolors which revealed his great talent. That is how trivial circumstances, although always unforgettable, were entered; the inva-
sion of the armadillo into the house, the hunt for a wildcat that was
devastating a henhouse, which had just started to yield after great
difficulty; the chasing away of Gallardo Lavalle's wild ostrich,
which had sneaked into the park in progress and had been pecking
at the few plants that survived the wind; the rides on ox-carts to the
nearest *boliche*[35]. Additionally he drew leaves of species he did not
know, plus designs to enlarge the house, plans for channeling work
and building of fences.

The exhausting routine of an *estancia* in the making filled the days
of the Larminats, men and women; the latter, between diapers and
baby bottles found time to make preserves, breed rabbits and chick-

[35] Boliche: A synonym for *pulpería*.

en, and contribute to the modest decoration of the house. A small corral was built to keep the dairy cow enclosed, and the first trees to provide shelter at the *estancia* were planted, with the idea of forming avenues gradually to improve the wilderness aspect of the surroundings. Those trees took a long time to grow, but the Larminats had a fountainhead that supplied water to the house, and allowed them the first successful plantings of flowers and shrubs, which at the end of that first summer were already coloring the scene.

Fall shortened the days' working hours, and soon the rains would come, the same as the first snow, around May 25. This national day was celebrated by the Larminats by hoisting both flags and saluting the rising sun with a salvo of eleven revolver shots, then to honor the *paisanos* with horse races, barbecues, cakes decorated with French and Argentine colors, *chicha*, pies, and a dance that continued until dawn. As the brothers had to admit: "Unfortunately in Argentina celebrations are an absolute priority, above any other occupation, and we saw many self-invited people who came to our *estancia* and did not hesitate to take things with them, even our tools; little by little we refused so much feasting". It also had to be borne in mind that the next day people were in no condition to work, due to the exces of drink.

It was not possible to overlook certain celebrations, because they meant a pause in the hard work. Aside from the national holidays, the end of the shearing was marked by a great lamb barbecue, followed by a dance; July 14, the French national day, was an occasion for joy with tricolor caps and ribbons; and of course baptisms and religious celebrations, in which it was possible for unwed couples to be united in matrimony. The Chilean national day was also commemorated, including a half day off. This was due to the evident influence of that country along the Andes of Patagonia, where Chile was more conspicuous, for its people and proximity, than distant Buenos Aires.

In October 1921 news of the wedding of Esteban and Geneviève de Montaigne de Poncins (who was a direct descendant of the philosopher Michel de Montaigne) arrived from France, with his intention of returning to Cerro de los Pinos in the coming February. Other news relating to European politics probably went unnoticed, but would have terrible consequences over the next two decades; Adolf Hitler had been named head of the National-Socialist Party, and in 1922 Mussolini marched on Rome and installed the Fascist régime.

In Argentina, an elegant *Radical*, Marcelo Torcuato de Alvear, who had been acting as Argentine Minister in France since the end of the war, was elected president of the Republic in 1922. The term of office of this "consummate Parisian" marked a particularly happy moment in the relationship between France and Argentina. Alvear founded the University of Paris Institute in Buenos Aires, the Argentine Universities Institute in Paris, the *Casa Argentina* within the Cité Universitaire in Paris, and promoted the Argentine Legation to the French government to the rank of embassy. And in his small château on the outskirts of Paris, "Coeur Volant", he organized reunions of Argentines with leading personalities of French politics and business.

The Larminats, in spite of their attachment to Argentina and their covenant with the country, kept in constant touch with their motherland. Subject to the way the post operated, they received French newspapers and magazines, aside from the family correspondence. The four families had agreed to take turns every two years to visit France, in sojourns that lasted from eight to ten months. The return of the travelers was a big occasion, among the presents and news that they brought books were most appreciated. Santiago read profusely, as he always had; all kinds of books on history, and novels, political and religious. They read the popular Jules Romain, Colette, they explored the surrealists, and both Magdelon and Santiago were devoted to Marcel Pagnol.

In May 1922, once Esteban and his wife –whom they called Youyou– were back and set up in their home, Santiago left for France to introduce his offspring, then represented by Bernardo, seventeen

215

months old, and Andrés, three months. The adventure to reach Zapala to take the train was, as always, hazardous. The automobiles that they rented for this journey were old and in poor condition, and the spare parts used for repairs were no more than a piece of wire. The road, as usual, was unpredictable. This time they left in two cars, one of which stopped dead after the first ten kilometers, and there they all stopped, to stay the night at Puttkamer's *estancia*, while the chauffeur tried to repair the gear box with a piece of wire, under candlelight. Next day they continued, but the breakdowns continued, and they had to spend several nights inside the car, with temperatures as low as eight degrees Celsius below zero. They arrived in Zapala five days later, when the train had left.

These complications, the growing families and the increasing expenses that the journeys to France involved, forced the trips to be made every three or four years instead of every two.

By 1925 all the brothers were married, and Santiago and Magdelon had five children, one of them a girl who died when she was one. Francisco and Magdalena also had five, one dead at one and a half; Esteban and Genoveva had two, and Roberto, who had married a sister of Magdelon in 1924, had his first daughter. Almost all the children had been born in the homes at Cerro de los Pinos, since the midwife came to the *estancia* and stayed on until after the birth. Sometimes she looked after two in-laws at the same time, who arrived together.

As for work, it had been organized in the most efficient manner, sharing tasks: Esteban was a born accountant, very disciplined, so he remained in charge of the bookkeeping and the cash, plus bills of remittance, branding and signals, business in banks, plans for fences and field measurements, apart from constructions on the Northern Estancia.

Francisco looked after construction materials and the building of fences, provisions, milling and general purchases. Roberto counted the cattle, grocery products (except the building and fences material), agriculture and grass fields north of the river. Santiago took care of

Collón Cura ferry

everything else, that is to say, orders to the foreman, farmhands, cart drivers and consignees; orders concerning the machinery; agriculture, construction and maintenance and the inventory of machinery and tools in the Southern Estancia.

The brothers had an excellent relationship, and they all considered themselves on an equal footing, but Santiago's strong personality and his ability to relate with neighbors and authorities was beginning to define him as the leader of the group. He had an extraordinary capacity to visualize the future, and was overflowing with ideas. While very active, he always declared that the success of the endeavor was due to all brothers in equal parts, and each contributed his own. A prudent disposition was that no member of the family could invade another's duties without previous notice; nobody could make an important decision without word to the others, and the tally and inventories of the products from the fields, and the animals, had to be communicated to the rest.

217

Soon after arriving with his wife, Esteban began to construct a new house on the northern margin, much more comfortable than the "Old Estancia" house, and in 1926 families moved in, his and Francisco's. This new house had a turbine designed and installed by Esteban, which supplied mechanical power and which allowed for certain luxuries, such as a model laundry and a cider factory. Using the power from the turbine a flour mill was installed, which turned out to be profitable, and remained so for many years. Oddly enough, electric lighting was not installed until much later, and they used a small wind generator, not the powerful hydraulic turbine.

As for the Southern Estancia, it had ceased to be a desert razed by the wind. There were trees accompanying the old *chacay*, and a kitchen garden that supplied asparagus, beetroot, green leaves, string beans, and some fruit. Some barns and the henhouse were constructed, and avenues were designed for the park. The two *estancias* exchanged products; if one was short of milk, the other sent some, getting back rabbits, pigeons and piglets. The families visited each other as frequently as the weather and the river permitted. Esteban was a great oarsman, and not only did he cross his family in a wooden boat, but in shearing time he was able to cross several times with bundles heavy enough to exhaust a rowing champion. As there was no communication between the houses on each side of the river, they invented a system to inform that one of the houses was inviting the inhabitants of the other to visit; it was a frantic flapping of white sheets. Also, until 1955, when a bridge over the Chimehuin was built, to get the wool packed in burlap sacks to the press on the Southern Estancia, it had to be crossed by rowing boat or in ox-carts.

The bad roads, the nights when they were surprised by the car breaking down and under the snow, the lack of communication with the post office, the heroic driving of herds to Chile, the difficult transport of wool in ox-carts, which had to travel four hundred and fifty kilometers along terrible roads, bordering the Limay up to the city of Neuquén, with little food and water for the oxen, which sometimes died before arriving; the complication of having the estate divided by a watercourse with ferocious tides, were all realities that took thirty or forty years to be modified. Many anecdotes of the early twenties were identical to others in the forties. The world was changing, but the *estancieros* in Patagonia achieved progress at a much slower pace.

12

The Thirties:
The Financial Crash

The September 1930 coup, in the streets

IN 1930 MY GRANDFATHER TRAVELED TO FRANCE with his family, which had grown to five children; the two boys, Bernardo and Andrés, and three girls, Jacqueline, Simone and Jeanine (there would be three more later). The trips to France had the feeling of happy anticipation, with the prospect of meeting again with family, and taking part in the summer get-togethers in the beautiful castle of La Hardonnière. But this trip had a special significance, above all for Santiago: shortly before, his father, Jean de Larminat, had passed away. My great-grandfather had always been very hospitable and affectionate with "his Argentines", and his absence would be felt. Furthermore, a number of practical details that would change the future of the Argentine undertaking had to be dealt with.

They left on March 29, 1930, and the first lap to Zapala to board the train, was as usual the most difficult. After a few kilometers, as was the rule, the rattletrap that was taking them broke down, near Puttkamer's *estancia*. There were several more breakdowns, and an equal number of repairs with a serviceable piece of wire, before they could board the ferry at Collón Cura, a short distance from the Chimehuin post office.

The ferry pilot, whose name was Oscar Morales, was a drunkard, who had short and few moments of lucidity. His wife, with the devotion due a better cause, did not let him go out when he was in a bad state, to prevent him from falling into the river and drowning. She would lock him up in the house, which was on the northern shore of the Collón Cura.

When a car arrived at the southern margin, as was the case with my grandfather, she answered the horn-blowing and revolver shots made by those who wanted to cross by standing sideways on a rock and making gestures with her right hand, moving her thumb down into her open mouth, to make clear that don Morales was not available and there was good reason for such a case. On that occasion the man's drunkenness lasted twenty-four hours, which forced my grandparents, helped by the chauffeur, to set up camp, cook a lamb and sleep on the bank of the river until the next day.

The next stop, one hundred and twenty kilometers from there, was the *estancia Catán Lil*, of the Zingoni family, where all passengers slept together in a large and freezing room. After innumerable mishaps they reached Zapala, where as was usual they enjoyed the hospitality of the Trannacks, an English family that had arrived with the railway and had established themselves at the *estancia El Manzano*. As time went by the second and third generations of Trannacks and Larminats became friends, to the point that children and grandchildren of don Arturo Trannack were part of the family for don Santiago's descendants.

Carrying on with their journey, don Santiago and his family took the train to Buenos Aires. At that time the trip took twenty hours, much less than in the fifties, after the railway was nationalized, when it took twice that time.

Furthermore, in the earlier period the train was comfortable and clean, with cabins of two and four berths, with linen sheets and woolen blankets, chinaware and silverware, all branded with the initials "FS" for *Ferrocarril Sud*, Southern Railway.

Once they arrived in France, they made the family visits they used to, and met old friends. My grandfather visited mates from the University and war comrades, such the selfless mechanic of his war tank, Tyrel du Poix. He also made use of the opportunity to apply through family contacts for a loan which would allow him a broader financial basis, to face the oncoming crisis. (That loan turned out to be extremely difficult to pay back in Argentina, due to the instability of the currency and domestic prices.)

But this visit revolved around the decisions to be made regarding the estate of the deceased father. There were long talks, especially with the *"petites tantes"*, the little aunts, who were the daughters of Jean de Larminat's second marriage, and it was clear that there had to be a change of emphasis in the family project. One of the brothers would have to return to manage La Hardonnière, and it was decided that it should be Francisco.

Francisco had expressed his desire to return to France, because his wife Madeleine suffered from a nervous ailment; she found that wind and isolation in Patagonia were unbearable. So a telegram was sent to him (via the Chimehuin post office) and Francisco embarked for France with his large family. As they crossed the Bay of Biscay carrying my grandfather back to Buenos Aires, the brothers exchanged messages greeting each other from ship to ship.

A few days later, my grandfather got the news that the vessel carrying Francisco and his family had collided with another and had sunk. They had to endure great anguish until the news arrived that all passengers had been evacuated safely. This episode was recalled in the family for a long time, arousing fears for what the tragedy could have caused.

Some years later another brother, Roberto, decided to return to France with his family, in an effort to cure the illness of his wife, Anne Doé de Mandreville, Magdelon's sister.

They left on April 1, 1934. Roberto, with his wife on a stretcher, feared with immense sadness that they would not meet again with those beautiful fall colors and that crystal clear atmosphere of the Andes. Anne died three months after.

Roberto rejected the idea of returning to Patagonia, a widower with six small children, and he chose to go to Lille to work for an oil firm belonging to the Wendell family. He later joined the army, returned to Paris in 1939 and there, in 1943, was married for the second time to Marguerite Mangin d'Ouince. After the wedding he went to the front, and was the only one of the Larminat brothers to fight in two world wars. This time he was seriously injured. Years after the war he was elected Municipal Counselor in Paris, and from that position he promoted the name of his adoptive country "Argentine" for a station of the Parisian Metro, beside the Arc de Triomphe. He retired to La Hardonnière, sharing the house with his brother Francisco.

The financial crisis triggered by the crash on the New York Stock Exchange in October 1929 did not leave a single country unaffected. In Argentina, the Larminats were seriously hit. One of the first consequences was the beginning of a long period of protectionism in the country, and the closing of the border with Chile, preventing the sale of cattle in what was the natural outlet for the calves and heifers that the *estancia* produced. The sharp drop in the price of raw materials, and particularly of wool, wrecked family finances, to the point that don Santiago asked if he should declare the partnership bankrupt. His children later said that he remained awake at night, walking about the room, making the timbers creak until dawn. However, he was able to weather the storm, and as from 1935 the rise in the price of wool and meat allowed him to regain wealth, and prosperity returned.

The crisis, the beginning of which had coincided with the death of their father, had as an after effect the departure of two of the brothers. The two that remained in Cerro de los Pinos had to multiply efforts to improve the efficiency of the enterprise. The trips to Europe became more sporadic, which meant a considerable saving. The perception that another war was near caused a new rise in the price of raw materials (the powers were building reserves of food and textile fibers), and the financial situation of the *estancia* began to improve.

In 1937 the Larminats undertook, with an enormous economic effort, the first geographical diversification, purchasing several thousand hectares in the district of Coronel Pringles, in the province of Buenos Aires, which meant returning to the original idea of growing grains.

The initiative was important; first, they were breaking out of a single family establishment in Cerro de los Pinos, and confirmed the Argentine aim of the project; second, for the first time they had available capital which exceeded the need of their families, a result of the management rationalization carried out after the departure of the two other brothers.

The new establishment was called *Pichi-Có*, and was managed by a distant relative of the family Des Francs, the efficient, honest and friendly Jaime Lockhart. Later, the multiplication of the estates was continued, buying other land in the district of Tornquist, and still later, hundreds of thousands of hectares of the *estancia Santa Nicolasa*, in the province of Río Negro, close to Chimpay. That was the same minuscule hamlet don Santiago had gone through when he went out to explore Patagonia for the first time in 1909, when he had to photograph, for the police commissioner, a man who had been assassinated in the local *pulpería*. This estate, the size of a small European country, charmed don Santiago. Setting up and populating that gigantic cattle business was no mean challenge, and herds of cattle were sent from Cerro de los Pinos to provide the new undertaking with the necessary means of production.

The children of the Larminat brothers began to grow in number and in age, in an atmosphere which, although influenced by the environment, continued to be tightly-knit and very Francophile.

After much thought was given to the education of the children and how to manage was discussed, it was decided to engage French governesses for the eldest. Adverts in French papers were published.

That is how the very severe Mademoiselle Nivault came to Cerro de los Pinos, to take charge of Santiago's children, and Madame Laforcade, of Esteban's.

Other governesses came later, such as the distinguished Mademoiselle Pavageot, Mademoiselle Marincovich, and Miss Pilar who, on both sides of the Chimehuin, contributed to give the numerous Larminats a solid education.

On Sundays after mass contests were organized to test the pupils' knowledge. Parents and governesses prepared the tests, and then formed the panel. The marks my grandfather gave the group have remained recorded in the *estancia* diary.

On one occasion he wrote: "Quite satisfactory, without excess". And some months later he had the pleasure of writing of progress: "Quite brilliant".

As from a certain age the older children began to move to Buenos Aires and were boarders at the Champagnat school (an institution belonging to Marist brothers, in Luján) and then the French School of Buenos Aires. This estrangement was tough for the "exiles"; from the moment they arrived in Buenos Aires they began to count the days to the summer holidays, the time to return to their beloved Cerro.

As from the decision by Santiago and Esteban to remain in Argentina, genuine efforts were made to establish relations with other families in the area and in Buenos Aires.

Furthermore, since Roberto's return to France (in 1934) both Magdelon and Geneviève each had their own house, without having to share. This new situation allowed them a better standard of living, and with it, the beginning of a more fluid social life. Before this, most of the visits were within the family; now they were open to a wider circle of friends.

Autonomy and economic prosperity also helped both families to improve their installations; more sheds were constructed, with new fences, canals, and a tennis court. Trips to Buenos Aires became more frequent, as well as stays in friends' homes. Visits have been record-

Don Santiago and Andrés

ed in the diary of the *estancia Tequel Malal*, of the Joneses', Ortiz Basualdo's *Península Huemúl*, don Bertil Grahn's *Mamuil Malal*, the Woods' *Huechahue*, Pim Larivière's *La Primavera* and Facht-Hohmann's *Collunco*, apart from old acquaintances such as the families Reid (*Gente Grande*) and Labadie (*Palitué* and *Toki Eder*).

Bonds were established or strengthened with the Mendaña, Trannack, Dawson, Brunswick of *Chacayal*, Taylor, and many more. In those visits Santiago enjoyed the company of his friends, and of good meals, but he never missed an opportunity to do business. He always ended up selling veterinary products and Cooper, Stewart & Co. machinery, which they represented, or else he bought wheat for the mill, sheep, or sold lambs or flour.

To complete the local integration, the Larminat brothers, in the person of Roberto, were part of the *estancieros* who founded the

229

Rural Society in Neuquén, which soon earned a reputation for grouping all the province's *estancieros*, apart from others who joined for social reasons. From its very foundation the Neuquén Rural Society became a spokesman before the government and the national professional entities such as the Argentine Rural Society. After some years, this society began to set up a show and annual gathering at Junín the los Andes, which became popular as a means of bringing together people from the whole of the province and from further away.

The creation of a stock of pedigree Australian Merino was started at Cerro de los Pinos, and for this purpose a thoroughbred ram, the famous B-616, was bought, paying the highest price on the market. They bought it from the Argentine Southern Land Co., which every year competed with the products of the Menéndez[36] estates for the big prize at the Palermo Rural Show. The ram had to be fetched by don Santiago at the *Maquinchao estancia*, and he did this in the company of his two sons, Bernardo and Andrés, then seventeen and fifteen years old. The boys wrote an entertaining report of that trip.

The three Larminats went in a rented Dodge pickup, with a chauffeur, and suffered the usual problems of the bad roads of those times. They crossed rivers by raft, got stuck in swamps, and broke down, until they finally arrived. The very large *Maquinchao estancia* was managed by a certain Mr. Dunlop, who with his wife welcomed the visitors with an urbanity and luxury to which the austere *estancieros* from Neuquén were not accustomed. There they met the pick of the Anglo-Argentine society from Buenos Aires, among them Mr. Gibson, representative of the River Plate Company, two Royal Air Force commanders who had come from the British base in the Bermudas with their own airplanes, and other British visitors. Don Santiago extracted from the bottom of his memory his rusty but very correct English, and the boys had a great time, although they had to sleep at

---

[36] Menendez: A large family from Chile, huge landowners and former colonizers of southernmost Patagonia.

the administrator's house, because the main one was overflowing with visitors. That was Bernardo's first close contact with the Air Force. He could not possibly imagine then that a few years later he would be fighting in the Canadian version of the uniform that those two elegant officers wore that evening.

About those years, between 1935 and 1940, the brothers undertook a project of importance, one they had been thinking about when they bought the *estancia* thirty years before: the construction of a bridge over the Chimehuin, the rebellious river that cut the estate in two, leaving them isolated for several months each year. The only exception to this was when somebody dared to face the tide, either on horseback if the level of the water allowed or in a rowboat, the latter demanding extraordinary skill and vigor. All heavy loads had to be crossed in ox-carts, and only when the river was ebbing.

The Chimehuin was not the only case; all rivers were important obstacles, since there were few bridges, and all communications depended on the level of the rivers. The post, which was so important for the family, arrived only when the river "gave way", which meant that the battered truck from the post office had to overcome all kinds of hazards to deliver its load.

In November 1935, one day when the river had a strong tide, the cable of the Collón Cura raft, by which went all the traffic of the valleys in the region, was severed in the middle of a crossing. The raft, carrying the post office truck at that time, was tossed by rough waters and crashed against a rock; the truck overturned in the river and several mailbags for San Martín de los Andes were lost. Among what could be saved was an envelope for don Santiago, from the wool dealer Angel Vélaz, with a check for a considerable sum, from the sale of wool of that year.

More serious than those accidents were the ones that took lives, and which had frequently cast families of the area into mourning for attempting to cross the *Chimehuin* when not advisable. My grandfather recalled with sadness the desperate letter that one spring day in

1931 his sister-in-law Geneviève had written to him, telling of the overturning of an ox-cart carrying two families with their children to the neighboring *estancia Chacayal*. The accident had taken place during the strongest tide, and the result of it was three children drowned; their little bodies had been recovered among the branches of the river late that night.

So the brothers Larminat felt justified in making a considerable investment to build a bridge over the Chimehuin. The challenge was not small, given the volume and vigor of the waters in winter and during the thaw, which turned the always turbulent but occasionally romantic course of clear water in summer into a raging torrent that dragged rocks, trunks and mud from the lakes and the slopes of the volcanoes in the Andes.

My grandfather left the calculations to his brother Esteban, an engineer, after agreeing that it would be made in wood, which was available and the traditional way to build bridges in the region and in Chile. While Esteban drew sketches and noted numbers, Santiago went for logistics; the purchase of materials, search for manual labor and engagement of two Chilean carpenters, Ibacache and Beltrán, plus their assistants.

Drawings were ready by the end of 1936, and as from January the next year the assembly of the bridge on the northern bank of the river was started, some two kilometers upstream from where the houses stood. The Chileans did a formidable job, fitting tongue-and-groove heavy beams made with cypress and *peyin*[37] oak from the Andes, little by little building the seventy-five meters long passageway.

The floor was made of thick planks, and the sides with a wooden reticulum similar to the metal railway bridges, which had to provide sufficient rigidity to bear the loads that would cross the bridge.

After several delays and contretemps, it was decided that on June 5 the bridge would cross the river. The water was swelling with the

[37] Peyín: Another of the southern Andean forest beeches, Nothofagus obliqua

first winter rains, although still allowing horses to cross by the usual fords.

That day, at eight in the morning, all the inhabitants of the *estancia* showed up at the works, close to which big fires had been lit to counteract the cold wind and also to prepare *maté* and some meat for breakfast.

Don Santiago, excited but also anxious, endlessly reviewed with his brother the schedule of the completion, a momentous event which would change their lives and make working with cattle much easier. The operation consisted of making the big wooden construction slide along its lengthwise axis, jutting the southern head of the bridge until it rested on the stone pillar that had been constructed on the other shore.

The stretch that the bridge had to cover in the air until reaching the other side was about fifty meters. It was a daring gamble, considering the limited means of elevation at their disposal and the material involved in the construction.

At last, in daylight, towards ten in the morning, preparations had been concluded. The farmhands in charge of the carts had finished tying the four teams of oxen, which were to drag the bridge on each side by means of cables and pulleys. The oxen had to pull the cables in the opposite direction to the way the bridge advanced, resting on wooden rollers, so that it would slide across to the river. Slowly, in an atmosphere of suspense, the far end of the structure, guided by two thick supporting cables, began to move. The oxen did not seem strong enough to progress at the speed expected, but the job was already under way.

Suddenly, when almost half the bridge was suspended over the river, a loud sound of cracking wood was heard, and the head of the bridge fell into the river, dragging the rest of the structure and dropping it in the direction of the tide. The audience, entranced by what they were seeing, were almost hit by the rear end of the bridge, which began to sweep the ground, forcing a group of women and children to run for safety.

233

The workmen managed to lasso and secure with cables the part of the bridge that had fallen into the river, and tied it to the oxen to bring it back to the shore. But my grandfather's brother, desolate, sensed that the damage was too great, doubting that the catastrophe could be remedied.

It was later confirmed that repairing the damage before the arrival of the high waters was impossible. It was never known if the cause was a particularly strong gust of wind, or if the bridge had a structural flaw and fell under its own weight. Through the notes written by my grandfather in the diary of the *estancia*, he seems to have come to the conclusion that there was a mistake in the calculations of the structure, which was not rigid enough and twisted as it was being moved, touching the water and so completing the disaster. The fact remained that the construction failed, and it was a traumatic experience for all. My grandfather, very much in line with his personality, insisted on reassembling the bridge, repairing the wreckage and correcting the weaknesses he had observed. But his brother, whom the experience had made overcautious, was in doubt. The carpenters (one of whom is called by an irritated don Santiago in his diary "a weeping Chilean") were obviously disheartened.

In spite of all the good intentions that year went by, and then another; and the re-launching never happened. Eighteen years later, in 1955, the objective was achieved when the Black Bridge was built, a totally different technical project.

Life on the *estancia* prospered, becoming more comfortable, at the same time as the social side developed. The families, their children having grown, began to visit their neighbors more frequently.

There was horse racing at don Santiago Labadie's, branding at *Huechahue*, polo games at the San Martín Regiment or at *Mamuil Malal*, visits to *Quemquemtreu*, and there was no shortage of guests from Buenos Aires, frequently members of the diplomatic service.

Don Santiago's two eldest children graduated with honors at the French College, but decided not to carry on in the University, dis-

The Black Bridge

couraged by the refusal of the Ministry of Education to recognize their French baccalaureate. So they went back to Cerro de los Pinos to work with their father.

The town of San Martín de los Andes, meanwhile, was undergoing transformation aimed at the still incipient tourism, especially fishermen who appeared with their strange bamboo rods for fly-fishing, almost all of them English or North American. For these guests the Dawson family opened a pleasant hotel with a big party, from which don Santiago's boys returned feeling under the weather, at the late hour of four in the morning.

Also in those years the Rural Show at Junín de los Andes grew, until it became an important celebration with riding contests, polo matches and games on horseback in which everybody participated, from middle-aged wives of *estancieros* to the young ladies.

Among the remarkable visitors of that time were the Minister of Yugoslavia, Mr. Kaderabec, the Minister of Serbia, ambassador Suli, as well as Mr. Tuck, the United States chargé d'affaires. With the latter my grandfather developed a great friendship; Mr. Tuck was so grateful for the hospitality at Cerro de los Pinos that upon returning to Buenos Aires he sent don Santiago two cases of one of the best Bordeaux, the Château Montrose 1921.

13

The Second World War,
Prosperity and Peronism

A Peronist meeting in Buenos Aires

WHEN THE SECOND WORLD WAR WAS DECLARED, clans were formed supporting either side. Obviously the Larminats, in the midst of the anxiety caused by their French relatives' isolation, aligned with the Allies, or the "French-British cause", as it was called, supported by their neighbors, particularly the Labadie, González, Mendaña, Dawson, Reid, Trannack and Wood families. As could be expected, von Puttkamer, the "old Burgrave", as don Santiago called him, joined the opposite side, and went to visit them "with an appalling *boche*[38] all marked by gas from the Great War, since he had fought at Verdun; both seem convinced of the rights proclaimed by Hitler".

News became a precious asset, the subject of conversation at every social gathering. On June 23, 1940, as soon as they knew of the "unexplainable treachery by the Bordeaux government" don Andrés Reid and his son went to Cerro de los Pinos to discuss it. Don Santiago, greatly disturbed but showing he had good knowledge of what

[38] Boche: A derisive term used in France to refer to a German, especially a soldier in the Great War.

was going on in Europe, placed all his hope on "this general, De Gaulle, who spoke from London five days ago". Bernardo, his eldest son, then twenty, had decided to join the Allied armies, but his father thought it was "impossible to let him leave yet, due to the uncertainty with which events are developing". Given the quick succession of actions, it was beyond all means to know then where and how to serve France best, without running the risk of making an irreparable mistake.

A little after, Don Santiago painfully wrote as his heading for July 14 in the *estancia* diary the words "National Mourning". France had been invaded and vanquished, and furthermore, the person leading the puppet government of what was left of France was Marshal Pétain, the same man who many years before had decorated Santiago with the Legion of Honor for his heroism on the front.

At any moment Bernardo would be called for his military service by the Argentine army, but he had other plans; he wanted to go to Europe to fight as a volunteer. Andrés, his second son, went to San Martín de los Andes to enroll as soon as he was eighteen.

The family decided to travel to Buenos Aires, and parted in August, in the midst of another cold winter, with the rivers overflowing with colossal flows, with snowstorms and hurricanes.

The Reids and a column of cars accompanied them to Zapala, always a tough road, even in mild circumstances, to help them if difficulties arose. They were able to get there, and then on the train with the families of Santiago and Antonio Labadie and his friend Geoffrey Wood.

Once in Buenos Aires, don Santiago put in motion all his battery of friends to ensure that his son Bernardo left for the warfront. He did not count, for obvious reasons, on aid from the French embassy, and neither from the Argentine authorities, who did not see eye to eye with their citizens wanting to fight for the Allies. The country had adopted a certain neutrality, but the government's sympathies were with the Axis.

Don Santiago was helped by French families against marshal Pétain's government, such as Zigler and Becquerel, and also ambassador Tuck, colonel Russell, from the British Army and the Canadian chargé d'affaires, Mr. Strong. Finally Bernardo got his ticket on a boat to New York and Ottawa, where he would join the Royal Canadian Air Force. Don Santiago wrote in his diary, laconically: "Ship, Brazil, Republic Line, 230 dollars + 10%". On September 28 his eldest son departed for the war, just as he and his brothers had done in the previous one.

Bernardo being absent, the management of ordinary tasks on the *estancia* fell to Andrés. Daily work was enormous: the work with sheep was interminable, because once the yearly round finished, the next one had to be started; dips against mange, the doses against parasites, eye-shearing, care of parturition, the rounding-up, selection of rams, and of course the shearing, the culmination of all efforts. Also the immense corrals needed maintenance, as did the hundreds of kilometers of fences, plus control of foxes and other offensive animals. In winter it was necessary to salvage sheep stranded in the snow; the prevention of robberies required being alert; there was need to plant trees, to keep the kitchen garden and the fruit trees, tame colts, buy and sell products from the country, trade actively with the other establishments in the region, keep meticulous records of stocks and commercial operations, manufacture flour almost daily, keep the mill, the canal and the hydraulic turbine working, make cider, ham...

My grandfather kept very active, and he even doubled his efforts. He reorganized the business in which he was a partner, obtained mortgages to finish paying for the new estate, and helped his youngest daughters with their studies, so becoming much closer to them. He also traveled frequently to Buenos Aires to make purchases, to sell the wool, and for inspection visits to the new estate in Coronel Pringles.

War carried on but it was like a stage play far away, not only because of the distance but due to the lack of news, since censorship applied to all correspondence allowed little news to come through. Sometimes don Santiago regretted the boredom caused by the absence of alternatives in the international situation. On one occasion, when a German neighbor whom he knew very well died, he was unable to overcome his unwillingness to go to the funeral: "First, I have no car, and second, I find myself enjoying my beautiful park too much to think about this poor *boche* who has died".

The family reaffirmed its unity around the patriarch, and they frequently got together with Esteban's family to spend a Sunday together, trying to alleviate the weight and uneasiness that Bernardo's absence caused in all of them.

In summer 1942, on February 14, the family decided to have a big celebration for the benefit of Free France. Everybody on the *estancia* worked hard to make it a success, inviting several friends to help. M. Chauveau, enologist in chief of the Trapiche wine company of the Benegas family showed up to help, with a donation of a number of cases of wine. The neighbor Geoffrey Wood also attended, proving himself a great guitarist and accordionist. On the appointed day nobody was missing; there were people from all the *estancias* supporting the Allies, the friends from San Martín and Junín de los Andes and even the odd *porteño*[39] that chanced to be there.

The entertainment was as follows: The Indian Pig Lottery, Don Ochoa's Auction, in which bottles of whisky and cognac given by the visitors were auctioned, Mr. McKay's Roulette, and music played by Magdelon and her daughters. After a magnificent lunch with all crammed into don Santiago's dining room, and when the weather refused to help and rain began to pour, the party continued with tea, and with French popular songs that they all sang in the patio of the house, while don Santiago's daughters went around selling programs with the lyrics of the songs illustrated by their father. The winners of the games donated their prizes back, and at the end some two thousand

---

[39] Porteño: A person born in or attached to the city of Buenos Aires. This term, when used in the provinces, often holds certain scorn.

pesos had been collected, which were sent to the Free France representation. As for the liquid prizes, they were totally consumed by those in attendance, who returned home feeling merry to an extreme.

Soon after Andrés began his military service at the Military Geographical Institute, and his younger sisters went to different schools in Buenos Aires, while Jacqueline returned to the Cerro, staying at the *estancia* to help her mother.

The modern and dynamic administration of their estates still occupied a great deal of don Santiago's time. The prosperity that his efforts yielded allowed him to buy more land in the province of Buenos Aires, which enlarged the *Pichi-có estancia*.

The 1942 fiesta was repeated in following years, always to collect funds. The pro-Allies neighbors, more and more satisfied as the Axis powers retreated, continued to cooperate with these events, and in each new edition donations increased. In 1944 more than six thousand pesos were collected.

In October 1943 a cable arrived from Montreal saying that Bernardo had been injured in Sicily, and that he had been promoted and decorated. They later received another cable signed by him in which he said his morale was high and that he had been promoted again. At the same time they received the news that the affable Geoffrey Wood had lost his life in a bombing mission. Bill Eddy, another man from the region, had also fallen, but fortunately, he eventually reappeared after hiding for two months beneath the German lines. Obviously neither don Santiago and much less Magdelon could avoid thinking about the immense risk that their eldest son ran in the Royal Canadian Air Force Spitfires and later on in the Free French Air Force. However, following a request by his second son, don Santiago did everything in his power to allow Andrés to go to the war. As soon as he returned from military service, his father began to press the new United States ambassador, Mr. Armour, the Canadian Minister, Mr. Kirkwood, and the British ambassador, to obtain a visa for Andrés. He visited them every time he was in Buenos Aires, he invited them and resorted to all manner of polite means to obtain what he wanted. Andrés, confident that these operations would succeed, stayed at *Pichi-có*, to be nearer when the visa as volunteer combatant was issued. His wish was fulfilled on June 20, 1944, when he left for the Canada.

The terrible 1944 winter prevented all postal communication with the *estancia*, but when the Collón Cura raft was able to cross and the post truck arrived, the family were able to read a cable by Andrés from Washington.

He informed them that he had arrived safely. They also received news from Bernardo who was on convalescence leave, having been wounded again when his airplane was brought down over the Adriatic. Andrés was sent to Algiers, from where he would go to France, to fight in the battle of Royan under orders of his uncle, general Edgard de Larminat, and later to Germany, forming part of a Free France unit in general Patton's American army.

In those years the situation was beginning to deteriorate in Argentina. There were no spare parts for machinery, gasoline and tires were rationed, and above all, the State was turning little by little into the hindering machine which it became in the end, hobbling all kinds of activities.

Among other more serious problems, *estancieros* were forbidden to make cider. This was the result of lobbying by the cider industrialists of the Río Negro valley, who concocted a series of applications and taxes to make production impossible for artisan cider makers. This was a loss for don Santiago, but, having become *criollo* in a way, and in spite of all the rules he continued to manufacture cider, but abstained from selling it.

In August 1944 don Santiago went with his brother Esteban to the Rural Show in Palermo. They had sent rams to the show which as usual meant an ordeal to get to Zapala to board the train, due to the great snowstorms of that year. The rivers rose so high that the famous 1927 record, when the water reached the maximum level in the region, was overtaken. Close to Esquel a formation of the narrow-gauge small train was blocked by snow for twelve days, and the passengers had to be fed by food dropped from an airplane. Two old people died in Lolog, buried by the snow; it was the worst winter in memory. At Cerro de los Pinos nine hundred and fifty seven sheep and seventy-three bovines died frozen or from starvation.

When they arrived in Buenos Aires Santiago and Esteban found themselves, on August 23, with the news of the liberation of Paris. Far from being alone in the celebration, the whole city joined in, with an enthusiasm that made them feel comforted. My grandfather described the celebrations thus:

"At midday Esteban and I go to Plaza Francia, where there are a lot of people chanting the Marseillaise. In the afternoon, the *porteños* meet spontaneously in Plaza San Martín, and by 6 p.m. an impressive crowd has gathered, with an indescribable enthusiasm. The police, obeying orders from a partially pro-nazi government, tries to restrain the rejoicing, without success.

"In the evening we go to the French Club on Rodríguez Peña street, and there I meet a regrettable group of old combatants, the typical morass of selfish and venomous people of the times before the war, in perfect contrast with the splendid demonstrations of Plaza Francia and Plaza San Martín.

"And on Thursday we returned to Plaza Francia, where we attended a new demonstration of over 100.000 people of every social condition and all ages, who sang the Marseillaise and the National Anthem. An Argentine demonstrator tells me: "Today, in Buenos Aires, we are all French".

"The newspaper *La Nación* printed this morning a Marseillaise in phonetic writing so that everyone can sing it. Absolutely everybody is holding the clipping, where the following can be read;

"Alons anfán de la patri ... i ... e
Le yur de gluar et arribé

Contre nu de la tirani... e
L'etanda... ar sanglan te levé
Antandevú dan no campañe
Muyir ce feroce soldá
Ki vie ne yusque dan nos bra
Egoryé no fis e no compañe...
Os ar... me situayén
Formé vo bataión
Marshón... marshón
Ken sangkempur
Abré... ve no siyón... "

"Absolutely colossal! Everything is very touching and the deep affection that Argentina has towards France is clearly felt, but it is also a demonstration against Perón. All kinds of songs are sung which at the end are against the pro-nazi government, like 'Argentines yes, Nazis no; San Martin yes, Rosas no; Democracy yes, Dictatorship no'.

"These are also heard: 'Adolf, Adolf, I told you clearly, you could not win against France' and 'Paris is again... one two three... Germans upside down'.

"With the pretext of preventing disorder, the police are continually producing a din with their sirens, attempting to charge with their horses against the demonstrators, and throwing tear gas. They are also bent on harassing the people who gather in cafés and restaurants to celebrate and sing the Marseillaise, but they go no further than that.

"On the next day I go with our lawyer to have lunch at the Harrods restaurant; beside us a large group of beautiful and very elegant young ladies are having a send-off for a bride. At the end of the meal they all stand up and sing perfectly three stanzas of the Marseillaise, and then the Tipperary song. Immediately all the people in the room get up and cheer them, including a table with senior officers among whom I recognized generals Tognazzi, Béistegui, Vadevalle, etc."

Another piece of good news that don Santiago received a few days later was that Elizabeth, the eldest of his brother Esteban's daughters, had become engaged to the Basque Andrés Laxague, to the greatest satisfaction of his parents and all the inhabitants of Cerro de los Pinos. It would be the first wedding of the second generation, and the launching of the third one in the country. From that marriage a stunning nineteen children were born, and over sixty grandchildren.

However, in spite of the considerable number of children that had been born from the marriages of don Esteban and don Santiago, that wedding was only the first of a brief series, and contrary to expectations, very few of the daughters of the founders got married. The warm family atmosphere, the comfort of remaining together at Cerro de los Pinos, and the lack of a true inclination in the family to develop a social life in Buenos Aires, made the other daughters of don Esteban remain single (three of them entered religion), and out of don Santiago's six daughters only Guillemette and Jeanine married. These two girls always had the intention of getting married, and did all that was necessary of their own initiative, eventually going to live in France to broaden their social circle, away from the isolation they were subject to on the *estancia*. But the sisters who remained at the Cerro de los Pinos were unable to find their blue princes locally. This was definitely a cost that had to be paid to maintain the pleasant life that my grandfather had managed to organize on the estate with his family.

That year the famous narrow gauge bridge over the Aluminé river in La Rinconada was inaugurated, a feat which called for a celebration with a barbecue consisting of nineteen cows and forty lambs, attended by the whole military high command and representatives of industry, commerce and banking in the region. That bridge was the beginning of the solution to the Collón Cura problem with the car-ferry. But the road to La Rinconada was atrocious, a fact that reduced the benefits. Don Santiago declared that it was an expensive solution, hardly practical, and that it would have been better to build a bridge close to the ferry, where access was much easier.

A little later, on February 25, 1945, don Santiago and Magdelon celebrated their silver wedding, in the absence of their sons but surrounded by their daughters, who gave them a marvelous song book bound in leather by Jacqueline and illustrated by all of them.

For Easter that year, Bernard was flying as a Captain in the prestigious Alsace squadron in the Free French Air Force and his Spitfire was shot down in Belgium by the Germans, though saving his life by using his parachute.

On May 5 don Santiago wrote with big letters in his diary: "General Capitulation in Europe" and set the whole family in motion to organize a big Victory celebration on May 10, hoping to get news of their sons, of whom they knew nothing. In June, don Santiago and Magdelon left for Buenos Aires, where there were continuous demonstrations celebrating the end of the war. The circle of 'Anciens Combattants' gave a cocktail party and a banquet in their honor, and don Santiago, with his unlimited energy, was able to collect an important sum in donations and goods for his cousin's 'Atlantic Army'. General Edgard de Larminat was still at the head of his troops, in a Europe hit by terrible famine.

The Allied armies were gradually being demobilized, and finally, at the end of September 1945 a telegram from the two brothers arrived at the *estancia*, saying that they were embarking on the *Désirade* in the port of Le Havre for Buenos Aires.

Don Santiago and his wife returned to Buenos Aires to wait for their sons, and met with a great political agitation caused by colonel Perón's race for power. In his diary, don Santiago mentions the unruliness, looting and violence never seen before in Argentina, produced by "thugs on Perón's payroll". This is the narrative by my grandfather of the arrival of his sons at the North Dock:

"October 18: General strike. We walk to the port, and pass by the railway station that we find closed, so we cannot meet with Guillemette and Jeanine, who must come from school. They are likewise unable to get a taxi, and finally arrive after walking 74 blocks.

At the port, where the entrance check points have disappeared, we simply walk in. A certain police officer issues the order that all of us waiting for relatives must leave, «because the boat shall not arrive today». However, at that very moment the *Désirade* appears at the head of the dock, immensely tall, floating like a cork on the water, because it is totally empty."

"The police evict us all just the same to make us buy entrance cards, which had finally arrived. Not so bad, I see Wladimir d'Ormesson coming, the ambassador of France, who was my desk mate at the Gerson school. We go in with him without any problem."

"Bernardo and Andrés arrive, without any noticeable change, other than their thinness. The boys manage to get their bags in spite of the strike, and don muftis. Members of the d'Hunval family are there (Bernardo's future wife will be Manina d'Hunval), but María Teresa Castrale (Andrés future wife) is blocked by shooting in the Avenida de Mayo, where the Peronists have set up a mortar in front of the newspaper *Crítica*, likewise defended by shooting back. Finally the Peronists burn down the newspaper, the machinery and the building. We move to the embassy of France, where ambassador d'Ormesson offers a cocktail in honor of the volunteers and their families".

It is easy to imagine the joy of the family at recuperating both brothers safe and sound. Bernardo, with his five years of war, brought a real load of decorations of the highest rank, English as well as French, plus all kinds of citations from his superiors. Andrés, who had a war of only one year, had also accumulated unforgettable experiences, as for instance when his regiment, the historic Moroccan Espahis First Marching Regiment, which formed part of general Leclerc's famous Second Armored Division (2ème DB), took Hitler's "eagle's nest", the Berchtesgaden castle in the Bavarian Alps.

All kinds of receptions, honors and parties were organized in Buenos Aires for the youngsters, who after a few days departed with their parents to their beloved Cerro de los Pinos. Once there life on the *estancia* was immediately resumed, as a laconic phrase in the diary the day following the return of the war heroes: "November 1. Andrés, rounding up the lambs, Bernardo with the calves of the Permanent square".

Shortly after ambassador d'Ormesson came to Cerro de los Pinos with his wife Conchita, and did not hide his admiration for the role played as volunteers by the two sons of his friend and former schoolmate, as well as the achievements by the family in the arid Patagonia. D'Ormesson was a cultured man, who wrote delightfully well and enjoyed talking with my grandfather about their memories of their teens and youth. They had lived in the exhilarating Paris of the beginning of the Twentieth Century, in which the unforgettable Belle Époque and Art Nouveau were in bloom, plus all the creativity of those years. In his memoirs, titled "From Saint Petersburg to Rome", published many years later and in which he relates his extensive diplomatic career, the ambassador recalls: "In Patagonia I met with my friend Jacques de Larminat, who was king in his land and his subjects were thousands of sheep".

In 1949 don Santiago experienced the joy of having his two sons marry their long time fiancées, Manina d'Hunval and María Teresa Castrale, and in the following year I was born, inaugurating with my cousin María Ana the series of twenty grandchildren that don Santiago and Magdelon would have. The attraction of the Patagonian land remains intact in me, since I still keep a house and spend a lot of time at Cerro de los Pinos.

On the *estancia*, the tradition of religious faith, so strong in the family, was never interrupted. The habit of inviting a missionary priest was maintained (for a long time it was father Zacarías, and later father Gruslin) to say mass daily for regular periods of four or five days running twice a month, attended by all inhabitants on both sides of the river. On holy days of obligation mass was sung in Latin, since everyone knew the Angels Gregorian Masses and the Sixth Tone Masses.

The sons return from the war

The family in full

The Cross on Cerro de los Pinos

Within that tradition the story of the cross of Cerro de los Pinos is inscribed, and has become an object of legend and a guidance point known by all in the area. The pupils from the Salesian College in Junín de los Andes make an annual pilgrimage to the top of the Cerro, and the cross is blessed many times a year by sportsmen priests who manage to climb the 1250 meters, where it stands.

The ancient dwellers of the area recall the story of the cross, which is the one the guides tell the tourists. It goes thus:

Before going to fight in the Great War, the four Larminat brothers decided to ask for divine protection, and for that purpose one day at dawn ascended the Cerro, each one carrying a cross made with cypress wood.

At the summit they planted the crosses and had them blessed by a missionary priest who used to come to the *estancia*. The pact that

252

they made was that upon returning they would bring down the crosses, and if someone did not return, his cross would remain up there representing him, at a site dear to all of them. It was not one, but two brothers who fell to German fire. The two that came back, don Esteban and don Santiago, complied with the promise of taking away their crosses, and with the two that remained don Roberto made a bigger one which he embedded on the top.

The definitive cross was placed and inaugurated for Christmas in 1925. My uncle Roberto had done the job with the help of the Ligers; this cross, made of cypress from the Andes, was almost five meters tall, and once placed could be seen from the four points on the compass, putting the valleys of the Chimehuin and Quilquihue under its protection.

Don Roberto's cross lasted over fifty years. After several repairs and some patchwork, the structure, worn out by time and exposure, was almost completely destroyed in the 70s by a ferocious wind storm, and its arms flew under a hurricane down the slopes of the Cerro.

In 1982 I had the satisfaction of replacing the remains of this monument with a new cross, to keep tradition.

This time it was six meters tall and made of steel, in cubic modules no more than 50 kilos each, so as to be able to carry them by hand to the top of the Cerro and assemble them piece by piece like a child's toy.

The cross was donated to me by one of my professors at the School of Engineering, engineer Augusto Spinazzola, who liked the story I told him and had the cross constructed in his factory. That is the cross that is seen nowadays, and which has already completed over twenty years resisting the wind and storms of Patagonian winters. In its interior I placed the wooden remnants of the first cross.

That is the tradition of the famous Cerro de los Pinos cross, and with that I put an end to my grandfather's story, also legendary and also real and which, the same as the cross, is a homage to Patagonia and to a man who felt more than anyone else a love for this land. His memory, the memory of his determined personality and his keen sense of ethics continue to hold strong in the generations that followed.

LAST NOTES

M̈Y DEAR GRANDMOTHER MAGDELON passed away at her home in Cerro de los Pinos in the spring of 1987. Of her two sons, my father Andrés chose to stay on in Cerro de los Pinos; he is still living there with my mother. My brother Pedro and I have constructed our own houses and we have the joy of seeing them often. My uncle Bernardo lives in the province of La Pampa, and his children are distributed all across the country and in Canada. Three of don Santiago's daughters, Jacqueline, Simone and Michelle, known throughout the region by their collective name "the Aunts" still live at my grandfather's house, which now had its turn to be called the Old House. Another of the aunts, Rosa Ana, is one of the few Larminats who live in Buenos Aires, and her two married sisters are still living in France. Such geographic dispersion does not prevent all of my grandparents' children from coming periodically to see their kin at Cerro de los Pinos.

The descendants of don Santiago and his brother don Esteban are over a hundred in Argentina, and have settled throughout the national territory. From Iguazú to the Beagle Channel, through the provinces of Misiones, Córdoba, Buenos Aires, Río Negro, La Pampa, Tierra del Fuego, the Federal Capital and obviously Neuquén, descendants of those pioneers can be found. Some have emigrated to other countries, and others have returned to France. The *estancia* Cerro de los Pinos, which meant so much to my grandfather, continues working well, and is still one of the most beautiful in Patagonia. Several of his children, grandchildren and great-grandchildren continue to live there, protected by the big trees which he planted and which multiplied by the thousand.

The huge herds of Australian merinos which were his pride are no longer there, because they succumbed to the low prices for wool, as happened in almost all of Patagonia. But they were replaced by thousands of Hereford cattle. On the other hand, the beauty of the place, its very clear rivers, its innumerable deer and its unique constructions have begun to be exploited for tourism, and each year hundreds of persons come from all over the world, to enjoy the purity of the atmosphere and the unpolluted beauty of the landscapes.

My great-grandfather's ambition to create in Argentina a new branch of the family has worked wonderfully, and is already the story of a success, similar to the story of so many European families that have come with their expectations and their energy to populate Patagonia and to form part of the Argentine people.

FAMILY TREES

Don Santiago's descendants

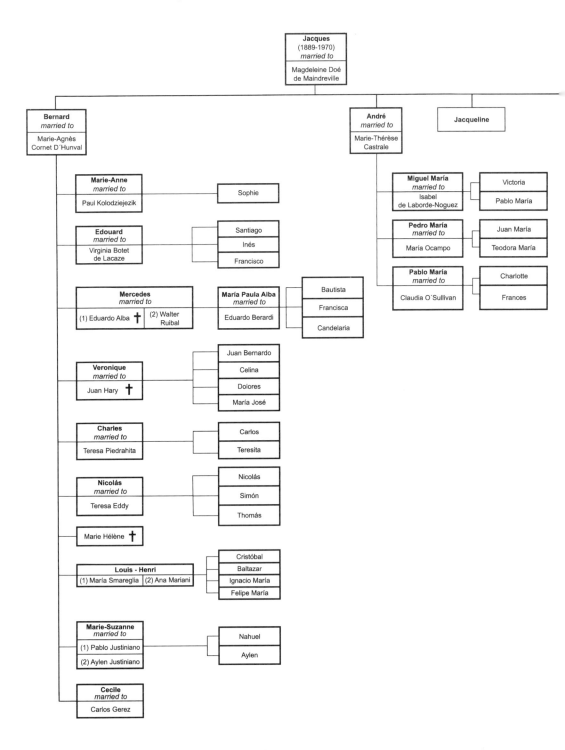

Jacques
(1889-1970)
married to
Magdeleine Doé
de Maindreville

Bernard
married to
Marie-Agnès
Cornet D´Hunval

André
married to
Marie-Thérèse
Castrale

Jacqueline

Marie-Anne
married to
Paul Kolodziejezik

Sophie

Edouard
married to
Virginia Botet
de Lacaze

Santiago
Inés
Francisco

Mercedes
married to
(1) Eduardo Alba ✝   (2) Walter Ruibal

María Paula Alba
married to
Eduardo Berardi

Bautista
Francisca
Candelaria

Veronique
married to
Juan Hary ✝

Juan Bernardo
Celina
Dolores
María José

Charles
married to
Teresa Piedrahita

Carlos
Teresita

Nicolás
married to
Teresa Eddy

Nicolás
Simón
Thomás

Marie Hélène ✝

Louis - Henri
(1) María Smareglia   (2) Ana Mariani

Cristóbal
Baltazar
Ignacio María
Felipe María

Marie-Suzanne
married to
(1) Pablo Justiniano   (2) Aylen Justiniano

Nahuel
Aylen

Cecile
married to
Carlos Gerez

Miguel María
married to
Isabel
de Laborde-Noguez

Victoria
Pablo María

Pedro María
married to
María Ocampo

Juan María
Teodora María

Pablo María
married to
Claudia O´Sullivan

Charlotte
Frances

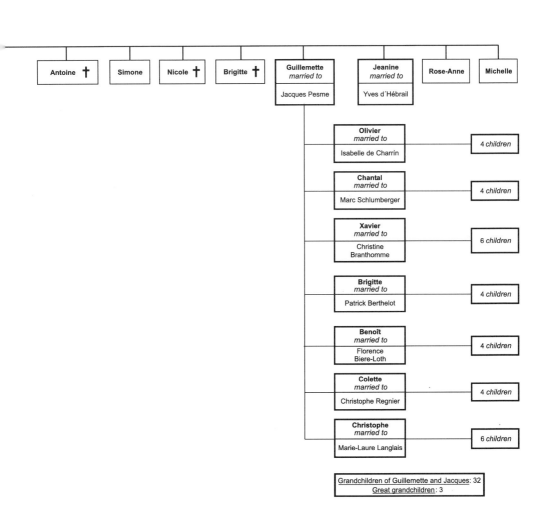

| | Antoine ✝ | Simone | Nicole ✝ | Brigitte ✝ | **Guillemette**
married to
Jacques Pesme | **Jeanine**
married to
Yves d´Hébrail | Rose-Anne | Michelle |

Olivier
married to
Isabelle de Charrín — 4 *children*

Chantal
married to
Marc Schlumberger — 4 *children*

Xavier
married to
Christine Branthomme — 6 *children*

Brigitte
married to
Patrick Berthelot — 4 *children*

Benoît
married to
Florence Biere-Loth — 4 *children*

Colette
married to
Christophe Regnier — 4 *children*

Christophe
married to
Marie-Laure Langlais — 6 *children*

Grandchildren of Guillemette and Jacques: 32
Great grandchildren : 3

Jean de Larminat's descendants

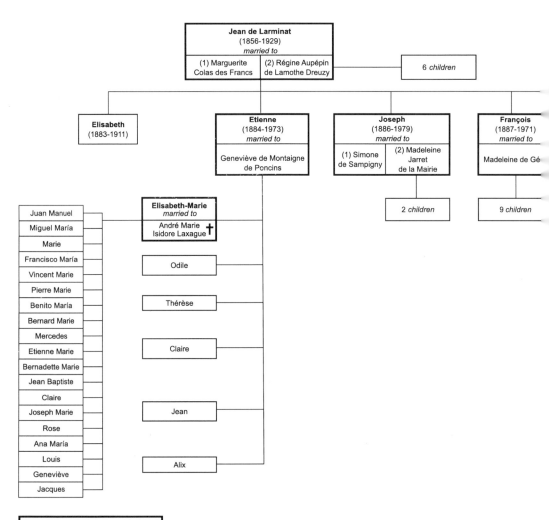

Jean de Larminat
(1856-1929)
married to

(1) Marguerite Colas des Francs | (2) Régine Aupépin de Lamothe Dreuzy

6 *children*

Elisabeth
(1883-1911)

Etienne
(1884-1973)
married to

Geneviève de Montaigne de Poncins

Joseph
(1886-1979)
married to

(1) Simone de Sampigny | (2) Madeleine Jarret de la Mairie

2 *children*

François
(1887-1971)
married to

Madeleine de Gé

9 *children*

Juan Manuel
Miguel María
Marie
Francisco María
Vincent Marie
Pierre Marie
Benito María
Bernard Marie
Mercedes
Etienne Marie
Bernadette Marie
Jean Baptiste
Claire
Joseph Marie
Rose
Ana María
Louis
Geneviève
Jacques

Elisabeth-Marie
married to

André Marie Isidore Laxague †

Odile

Thérèse

Claire

Jean

Alix

Grandchildren of Elisabeth and André: 70
Great grandchildren: 6

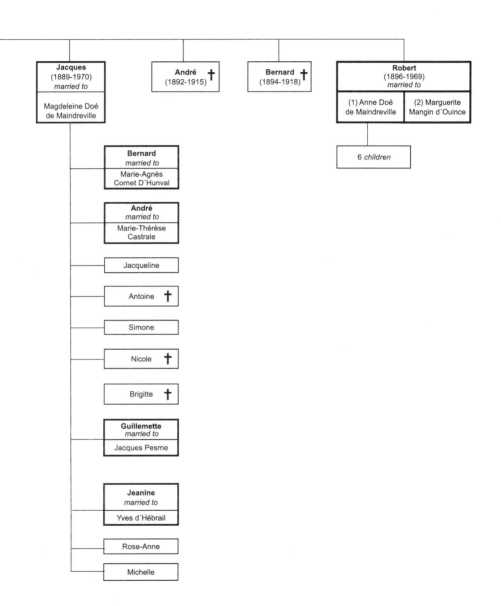

Jacques
(1889-1970)
married to

Magdeleine Doé
de Maindreville

André ✝
(1892-1915)

Bernard ✝
(1894-1918)

Robert
(1896-1969)
married to

(1) Anne Doé
de Maindreville

(2) Marguerite
Mangin d´Ouince

6 *children*

Bernard
married to
Marie-Agnès
Cornet D´Hunval

André
married to
Marie-Thérèse
Castrale

Jacqueline

Antoine ✝

Simone

Nicole ✝

Brigitte ✝

Guillemette
married to
Jacques Pesme

Jeanine
married to
Yves d´Hébrail

Rose-Anne

Michelle